BECOMING A
DIGITAL UNICORN

5 Steps to Set Yourself Apart in a Competitive Economy

TRICE JOHNSON

HybridGlobal
PUBLISHING

Published by
Hybrid Global Publishing
301 E 57th Street
4th Floor
New York, NY 10022

Manufactured in the United States of America.

Johnson, Trice
Becoming a Digital Unicorn: 5 Steps to Set Yourself Apart in a Competitive Economy
    ISBN: 978-1-951943-67-7
    eBook: 978-1-951943-68-4
    LCCN: 2021907455

Cover design by: Jonathan Pleska
Cover graphic design by: Dean Williams
Author photo by: Bryan Medina
Copyediting by: Claudia Volkman
Interior design by: Suba Murugan

Legal Disclaimer:

www.realdigitalunicorn.com

ACKNOWLEDGMENTS

To the millions of people around the world who lost their jobs during the 2020 pandemic and will never see the return of their occupation because these jobs have been replaced by automation, may this book bring you hope and steps to pivot to your future.

To the youth of our world who are exploring non-traditional career paths, may this book spark creative inspiration and provide you with new ideas to prepare for the digital workforce.

To everyone who has been told that you will not be successful in this new economy, may this book be the key to unlock the dreams and talent hidden within you and unleash new levels of boldness that empower you to dominate the times.

To my Heavenly Father who breathed life into this project and made this book possible.

To my dad, the late Willie Johnson, may your soul be at rest and peace in your heavenly home.

To my husband, Shawn, who pushed me to keep going and brought me laughs and encouragement every step of the way. To my mom, brother, and grandmother, Gwen, Kedrick, and Phyllis, who always believed I could achieve more even when I didn't, and who have been an incredible & loving support system my entire life.

To my God-Family the Barton's & Jones, Taneshia, Ernest, Camelia, and Glen, who helped me to unlock new levels of greatness through their fervent prayers and continue to shower me a tremendous amount of love each day.

To my in-laws, Gail, Sandy, Alice, and the rest of the Gipson family, who gave me great advice and positive inspiration throughout my book-writing process.

To Karen, Ishq and other amazing friends, family members, and colleagues who motivated me continuously, I am eternally grateful.

CONTENTS

PART III: DELIVER IRRESISTABLE VALUE EVERYWHERE

PART 1: BECOME YOUR OWN UNICORN— STAND OUT IN A CROWDED ECONOMY

To do something new, *you* must become new.

This is true now, more than ever. The rapid speed of technological change is forcing many of us to rethink our career paths, update our skills to keep pace with future work, and increase our digital capacity.

Most of the physical world has already been explored and mapped, but the digital world remains an open one—with infinite potential and countless, untapped opportunities. And no matter where you currently are in your life or career, you have full access to explore the digital world and make your mark.

As the economy continues to change, it will be a requirement for each of us to design new strategies to adjust our skills and boost our adaptability so that we can pivot and adjust quickly when these unexpected changes occur. And as technologies such as artificial intelligence (AI), machine learning (ML), and the internet of things (IoT) continue to become more pervasive in our daily lives, we must go beyond the general understanding of these terms to translating these technologies into new ideas that solve relevant problems today and unforeseen problems tomorrow.

For example, AI and ML played a leading role in the fight against COVID-19. Scientists around the world relied on advances in computing power and AI to transform and interpret mass volumes of data into simulations that accelerated our understanding of this highly contagious virus. Prior to the 2020 pandemic, it took many years for a vaccine to be delivered to market. In fact, the fastest vaccine to go from development to application was the mumps vaccine in the 1960s, which took approximately four years to complete. Because of advances in AI and machine learning, medical research companies like Pfizer, Moderna, and Johnson & Johnson were able to deliver vaccinations globally within eight to twelve months. The 2020 pandemic resulted in severe global social and economic disruption, causing millions of job losses around the world with more than 42 percent of these jobs never returning.

Your unique innovative spirit is needed now more than ever. Your ability to think beyond what's possible is what makes you attractive to companies. Sharing a new lens on a problem and a fresh perspective demonstrating how companies can differentiate themselves in the market is what makes you so attractive to them. To be unique and set apart in the digital world requires more than just the ability to code or the skills to write instructions for a computer program or application. For the majority of my career, I didn't know how to code; when the GitHub code repository was invented, it gave me a way to leverage other people's code to build really cool software applications that I couldn't have developed on my own. To my core, I am a strategist, architect, innovator, and painter of dreams – not a developer. So, I guess that's the motivation for this book. I want you to discover your unique mark in the digital world; one that will allow you to explore many paths to success in this digital economy. The digital world is your blank canvas waiting for you to create your own unique masterpiece.

I know that my success in the digital era is attributed to the fact that I've doubled down on cultivating my unique abilities, especially my human competencies to have an empathetic mindset, high emotional intelligence (EQ), an ability to effectively communicate, a growth mindset to navigate change, the gift of being continuously curious—and most importantly, strategic analysis and analytical thinking abilities that help me to solve highly complex problems. These are the characteristics that continue to accelerate my career in digital spaces—not just understanding the technology. It's leveraging a critical set of meta-skills that make me more adaptable when it comes to uncertainties or future disruptions and the marketplace.

So, it's not only important to understand the implications of the technologies related your career; it's also how you can invent the next big thing through your creative mindset. This is demonstrated by the inventors of AutoX, the first autonomous grocery delivery and mobile store service in Silicon Valley with self-driving cars. Customers order their items through a mobile app from an online grocer that works directly with producers, eliminating the need for stores. Then AutoX uses self-driving vehicles combined with AI software, sensors, and real-time cameras to deliver the groceries, while providing customers with the ability to browse their vehicle-based mobile store upon delivery.

These advances are fueled by:

- an increasing number of smart devices collecting, analyzing, and sharing data
- the computing and processing capacity of computers reaching double figures every two years
- the mass variety of devices connecting to the internet each day
- our accelerated journey to create and access oceans of data online globally—more than 200 zettabytes by 2030 to be exact

These digital leaps forward are drastically improving the world for businesses, increasing productivity for workers, creating better experiences for consumers, and bringing more creative products to the marketplace.

What does this mean for you?

Although technical skills such as computer programming or coding are highly valued in the digital economy, innovation and advances in SaaS (Software-as-as-Service), Low-Code, and No-Code apps are opening new doors for corporate and entrepreneurial enthusiasts to solve complex business problems without the need to code, have a computer science degree, or complete multiple years of deep technical training. The world of SaaS and low-code/no-code are becoming available to people who previously would have been challenged to get a foot in the door of large tech firms or vertical/industry-driven organizations without a software engineering or computer science degree, or the ability to code.

Think about how YouTube and Vimeo democratized video content creation for creators who have never filmed for a professional studio or spent millions of dollars on equipment to create high-definition, entertaining videos for web audiences. The ability to quickly build mobile apps, web apps, or chatbots through easy click, drag-and-drop building blocks means that you can focus more intently on developing your innovation, creative thinking, and learning skills if coding is not your niche.

In the digital world, barriers to this economy are being lifted, and companies are making it possible for anyone from any background to have access to roles that were inaccessible without a four-year technical degree. Now is the time for you to consider your career pivot and leverage the vast volumes of research and courses available online. Today's needs are great with no shortage of problems to solve—and the digital universe is wide open.

Where you go, and how far, can largely—if not completely—be driven by you.

ONE

The Age of the Digital Unicorn

Aileen Lee, a venture capital investor, first used the term *unicorn* in a 2013 *TechCrunch* article to describe the rare occurrence of privately held startups that were valued at over $1 billion. Today, this term is used to describe anything, across a wide range of disciplines, that proves to be rare, iconic, and magical.

Similarly, a Digital Unicorn is a rare individual who—through their digital skills and capacity—exceeds expectations, takes businesses to the next level, and performs above the highest standards when faced with uncertainties about the future.

Digital Unicorns set themselves apart from ordinary individuals on a continual basis. They have learned to master digital skills, ranging from the most basic to the most complex—and people love being in their presence because of the immense value that they bring to the table.

A Digital Unicorn is a person from any industry, experience, culture, or background who has the remarkable ability to find, analyze, utilize, share, and create ongoing value for others, using technology and other related capabilities, including:

- advances in cloud computing
- business and mobile apps
- social media
- data and analytics
- business intelligence
- network and security
- digital design thinking

Consider this book your digital masterclass, designed to increase your capacity as a Digital Unicorn so you can become a unique influencer in your industry, domain, or business. It's time to replace outdated habits and behavior patterns you may have developed over the years that would get in the way of you reaching your highest digital capacity. This goes beyond accessing files on Google Drive or creating a Word document, designing a presentation, tweaking code on a website, or blogging on social media. Instead, you have cultivated an approach to future-proof your skills and increase your value to organizations by activating your multiple intelligences through a high growth mindset, embracing a new set of skills that sets you apart from the pack—emboldening you to differentiate and distinguish yourself. While you continue to personally transform, know that your path to success can only be completed once you help others and are willing to collaborate, extend a hand, and serve others who are discovering their purpose and place in the digital world.

Discover Your Own Uniqueness

I believe that each of us are born with unique gifts and talents to deploy to the world. We each possess a uniqueness that sets us apart from others. There is remarkable value in cultivating your unique brand. You can leverage your personal brand to empower businesses and communities and create positive change in the world. During this masterclass focused on becoming uniquely and invaluably digital, I will walk through five steps to set yourself apart and discover your inner Digital Genius. How will you get there?

- By making a hunger for knowledge a lifelong pursuit

- By distinguishing yourself from the rest of the crowd through your unique gifts and expertise
- By renewing your skills as a deliberate, daily practice
- By offering a fresh perspective that only you can bring
- By being flexible and adaptable
- By turning your unique ability to connect the dots into something other people seek you out for—and compensate you generously for
- By making your unicorn leadership spirit an invaluable asset, not just to businesses and communities—but to the world.

Just like the beautiful, mythical, one-horned creatures they're named after, Digital Unicorns are rare.

In other words, they are *unique . . . set apart.*

When you maximize your potential and have a capacity for heightened intelligence and understanding, you accelerate your ability to see with a different lens. As a result, because everyone has something unique and differentiated about them as an individual, you will see what others can't see, and you will be able to help business and leaders uncover new opportunities that have yet to be imagined.

How incredible is it to be able to bring a unique intellectual energy and perspective about the digital space that no one else can bring but you—or ever fully duplicate! When we collectively bring all of our unique insights together, we can help business leaders by solving problems and creating innovation—and we can also empower and inspire everyone around us in the process.

I'll let you in on a secret: That value is *already* inside of you.

Your goal is to tap into and understand your own uniqueness, and then do the research and deep learning to deliver a fresh perspective on what's going on in the world and how that is impacting companies, influencing societies, and shaping the future.

We each fully unleash our inner unicorn when we discover something really unique and special about ourselves. This is the part of us that we should *never* turn off—even as we accelerate our learning and continue to grow.

The key is being able to cultivate and strengthen something unique about yourself that can add value to the people around you—and even benefit people you may never meet. It's our individual gifting—our gift to others and the world.

Questions for Reflection

- What are the unique gifts that distinguish you from the rest of crowd?
- What fresh perspective can you share with your world?
- In what ways do you demonstrate being flexible and adaptable?

TWO

Disrupt (Yourself) Before You're Disrupted

The concept of disruption was first linked to products and services describing an approach that enables a smaller company with fewer resources to successfully challenge established businesses that have greater resources. These smaller companies or new entrants become disruptive when they begin to successfully target markets with products and services that have been overlooked, disregarded, ignored, or unseen. As I've navigated my career over the past couple of decades—taking bold and unusual paths, I believe that following the business principles for disruption has been a major advantage for my career. On a personal level, to disrupt yourself means trying something that's never been done before, challenging the status quo, or questioning an established set of standards.

You must be willing to quit the right stuff at the right time and understand when to pivot. Unpredictable change and uncertain times present opportunities for you to pause, think deeply, reset, and disrupt yourself to change the rules of the game. Be prepared to alter the events in your career that are fading to breathe life into new ones that will cause you to transcend the era of uncertainty. You must continually evaluate ways to disrupt yourself before you get disrupted and left behind.

For me, this means going beyond my usual pivot. Disrupting myself must be a part of who I am at my core. For example, I had been a consultant and technical architect for more than a decade of my career. I realized that for me to move to the next level in leadership—which in my case was to become a strategic leader focused on strategy and innovation—my technical architecture skills required a disruption. This did not mean I needed to throw away my skills and ignore their existence, but it did mean that I needed to change the habits in my life to cultivate a new set of skills.

I began to do some deep research, and I took numerous online courses to get certified in areas of strategic thinking and business innovation. I leveraged my background as a cloud architect with system design and architecture skills to help me understand how to connect the dots for strategy and innovation projects. Then I completely altered my path and stopped applying for architecture roles. I started only interviewing for roles aligned to the strategy and innovation leadership path. I also requested executive stretch assignments from my mentors, which meant taking on extra work on weekends and evenings that had nothing to do with my current role. However, this elevated me to a new paradigm in the strategy and innovation space. I also cultivated and grew my new skills by volunteering my time at various nonprofit organizations and start-up companies, helping them with their strategic planning and innovation strategies at no cost and deploying my gifts to communities and businesses who needed them.

This is how you disrupt yourself year after year—by elevating your skills, going deep in specialized knowledge, quitting the things you should quit, and pouring yourself into the areas that require the gifts you have to offer.

Today, all industries are going through some level of digital transformation. As we continue moving through the Fourth Industrial Revolution—which Wikipedia defines as "the ongoing automation of traditional manufacturing and industrial practices, using modern smart technology"—every company will become digital.

Every company will harness digital technologies to create and deliver new sources of value for customers and increase employee productivity. Companies will also encourage the creation of digital cultures that help distinguish their company from others, deepen customer and partner relationships, and deliver increased growth, profitability, and success.

So, what does this mean for you?

It means you are reinventing at the right time.

Emerging technologies are being applied in new ways as the virtual world continues to merge with the physical world. We all must tap into our inner three-year-old selves to take on new adventures where we are not afraid to explore, experiment, fail fast—and bounce back rapidly. As you reflect on your journey to transform and expand your gifts or start a new digital career, you must walk boldly and with courage through the uncertainties. You must take on this fearless journey to help new businesses emerge, empower companies to reinvent how they do business, and create entirely new products and services. And if you're an entrepreneur, the company (or companies) you're transforming are your own. To solve many of the greatest challenges in this era and shape the future of digital businesses, you must have an innovative spirit. You must be able to connect the dots and influence decision makers—and become a leader in your own right.

This involves cultivating new habits and developing a digital mindset that allows you to think and to look at problem solving differently.

However, you can't transform your mindset if you haven't dealt with your self-perception and attitude.

Having the attitude of a digital being means having beliefs like these:

- I am an innovator.
- I am the best at what I do.
- I believe there are opportunities all around me.
- I am confident.
- I am bold.
- I am excited.
- I have an attitude that is energetic.
- I have an attitude that is positive and infectious and energizes everyone around me.

It means asking yourself key questions like these:

- What am I doing daily to cultivate myself and tap into the limitless opportunities around me?
- How am I harnessing the power of technology in order to see things differently, take in data from many different sources, and be able to use that data to make informed decisions faster and help companies to be able to see patterns more quickly?
- How do I make all these things work together?

In this modern era, digital literacy, talents, and skills are the top survival skills that will help you to solve some of the most complex problems in the world and engage in the most in-demand, emerging digital tasks. I've seen many careers get disrupted in a negative way, especially during the 2020 pandemic. Now is the time. You have an awesome opportunity to begin to reinvent yourself by reskilling, upskilling, and staying relevant, regardless of major market and social shifts.

I want you to re-channel your energy—particularly if you're feeling left behind, feeling that technology has moved on without you and that robots are here to replace you—and realize that you can reroute your future into positive, fertile territory. Shift all the energy that's not beneficial and translate it into fuel for your journey to become digitally intelligent and deeply innovative. As a result, you'll be able to help innumerable business that need your innovation and intellectual energy.

No more feeling sorry for yourself! Those days are done.

The path for entering the digital world is wide open, and it's time for you to discover your seat at the table and sit right down with boldness and confidence.

Today, there's a new shift happening in our digital and service-focused economy. Rapid skills transformation is top of mind for leaders who are accelerating their business transformation. This urgent change is placing pressure on individuals and entrepreneurs to acquire new knowledge and skills more rapidly, and in some cases, transition entirely into new industries.

The world is changing at a rapid pace due to digital innovation, and if you don't personally reinvent yourself by increasing your digital intelligence, you will become displaced or irrelevant, similar to businesses who fought change and no longer exist.

Blackberry's RIM smartphone failed to keep pace with Apple's and Googles' speed of innovation. Brick-and-mortar bookstores like Barnes & Noble continue to struggle, as well as experiencing significant revenue losses as they grapple to keep readers who have abandoned physical stores and now purchase their physical and downloadable books from online platforms like Amazon.

Then there's the infamous Blockbuster story, where the video giant refused to transform to digital streaming services while its competitors, like Netflix, focused on reimagining video rental in the digital age through new and innovative approaches.

When companies design their business models without leaving room for transformation or paths to reinvent themselves, the results are their irrelevance at best—and their demise at worst. Like the company histories I just shared, what happens to those who resist change provide well-documented cautionary guidance.

My husband, Shawn, and I are considered career pivoters as annually we assess the marketplace, look at all the patterns around us, and make decisions about the next professional move required to keep us relevant. For example, Shawn was an accountant and financial analyst for most of his career. As big data and data insights and visualization became more relevant for businesses, we knew that it was an opportunity for Shawn to pivot his career. So he proactively took many online courses to get his data visualization certification across a few platforms such as Tableau, Qlikview, and Power BI. Within a year, we witnessed a complete personal transformation in Shawn's skills that immediately qualified him for next-level digital roles in this new economy. The types of roles he qualified for began to rapidly shift from accounting and finance to data visualization. The two of us have made learning a lifelong path and personal transformation a continuous requirement in our lives to keep our skills in demand in the digital economy—and beyond.

You can get this kind of information and training through many online sources, including YouTube videos and cost-effective courses on the learning platform Udemy. You can also take a Massive Open Online Course (MOOC) through any major institution of higher learning, or through leadership or executive training. These are all ways you can begin to write your blueprint to reinvent yourself to become a digital force. For more than twenty years, I have always taken alternative paths for lifelong learning. I didn't finish my college degree until my late thirties, and I did so through an online college program whose accreditation was less than stellar. However, I've always had a passion for learning—particularly on emerging topics and trends in the technology field.

Every six months I scan the global markets to understand the needs of leaders and what's important and top of mind for them so that I am better prepared in my own personal transformation journey to align my passion, gifts, and purpose to the needs of these leaders.

Remember: disrupt or be disrupted.

The key is having a framework that provides a simple, actionable approach to get to your destination. And that's the journey we are going to take to enable and empower you, no matter where you're at in your life or career, to reinvent yourself so that you can help to shape and lead the digital economy.

Questions for Reflection

- What limitless opportunities do you see around you right now?
- In what ways are you tapping into these opportunities?
- What are the top three ways you harness the power of technology in your day-to-day life?

THREE

Checkmate! Win at Digital Disruption

A checkmate in chess is a game-ending move to win. In order for you to be successful in the digital world, you must understand your own game-ending move . . . the fulfillment of your purpose. Then, just as with a winning chess strategy, you must activate the patterns required to prepare, cultivate, execute, and win in this new economy. An effective chess strategy involves the study of checkmate patterns. When a player successfully puts their opponent in checkmate, they win the game. Good chess strategy involves studying many different checkmate patterns to prepare to execute or defend against them.

To stay ahead of the market and be part of technology's next wave of digital disruption, I continually transform and reinvent myself through a personal framework that enables me to succeed beyond the current times.

I have worked with hundreds of global leaders across corporate industries, governments, and educational institutions, as well as with entrepreneurs. They all share the same passion during these unprecedented times of digital disruption to not just survive—but thrive!

I have worked with business and government leaders who have courageously guided their companies through global recessions; bubbles (where a market is hot—until it's *not*); international political crises; and other kinds of social upheavals and natural disasters.

Through every one of these historic events, these leaders were forced to transform and reinvent their companies and their people in order to emerge from the ashes, persevere, and succeed. These leaders depended on consultants and entrepreneurs like me who could see problems and solutions with a uniquely cultivated "outside-in" lens. Guess what? I can be you—and you can be *me*. You also have a digital mindset and incredible value to offer companies and leaders.

As I help business leaders to reinvent themselves and their companies, I have always understood the importance of my own personal transformation as the secret sauce that helps me to stay steps ahead of market change and stay relevant. This enables me to help lead businesses to their new, and greater, destiny.

My personal experiences and my expertise will provide the masterclass format for this book. I will also draw from hundreds of conversations with C-suite business leaders (that is, CEOs, CFOs, CTOs, etc.) and others about large-scale, global projects. Areas of focus include artificial intelligence (AI) and machine learning (ML); big data; Internet of Things (IoT); intelligent robots; robotics process automation (RPA); blockchain; intelligent platforms; and other emerging technologies. Don't be intimidated by these tech terms if you've never heard of some—or all—of them. With a simple click of a button, you can access thousands of pieces of online content that will explain each of the terms much better than I can. That is not the purpose of this book. I want to motivate you to think differently and cultivate a unique path for your career that allows you to stand out—and sets you apart from your peers . . . and even your competition.

In order to help my clients, I had to understand the transformation journeys they had taken thus far. This was necessary for them to effectively adopt emerging technologies. But even before that, I had to take my own *personal* transformation journey so I could influence these businesses and startups to become digital. As businesses of all kinds are going through deep transformations to become more digital, their ability to do so first depends on cultural transformation. That's why your own personal transformation is so important as well—and it starts with shifting your mind.

There are a few important things to understand about what it means to *become digital.* The first thing you need to know is that it's *not* about mastering technology. However, it *is* about:

- Adding value to businesses that need your innovative spirit
- Making yourself digitally aware so you can define your purpose and your place in this digital world
- Becoming digitally intelligent so that you are not left behind professionally
- Increasing your digital competencies so that you can survive and thrive in this competitive digital landscape

A mind shift of embracing *constant* personal reinvention is also necessary in order not to be impacted negatively by changing times. I'll show you how and why resetting your mindset will help you to overcome and move beyond the uncertainty that typically follows change—in order to thrive and win.

This book will take you through a five-step, personal transformation approach that will start your journey to become a Digital Unicorn. When those around you can't give you the guidance you feel you need to be successful, the one thing you can have is a consistent personal framework that inspires you to personally transform—not only when necessary—but often. The timeless principles I share here can provide you with you a steady foundation to help make you extremely valuable to—and sought after by—employers and clients. This book will guide you to make wise and thoughtful decisions that can help you do everything from setting yourself apart to land your first job (if you're just starting out) to having a long and prosperous career—despite not knowing what will happen next in this rapidly changing digital world.

Questions for Reflection

- In what ways can you add value to business who are looking for new ways to innovate?
- What are some practical ways you can increase your digital competency?
- How have you reinvented yourself so far in your life?

FOUR

You've Been Framed

In order to transcend difficult times, we must have a framework for resilience and recovery. Our personal transformation framework enables us to rise above the times and any circumstances we find ourselves in. This is critical since we can't always predict how or when technological advances will interrupt or disrupt our personal and professional lives. How do you transcend—or rise above—the macro and micro implications of digital advances? What is your plan to recover, transform, and reinvent yourself? Having a framework can help you do just that.

Believe it or not, even if you read this book for the first time in 2025, *all* of us will still be experiencing the ripple effects of changes ignited by COVID-19. Think about it: When you decide to travel by plane, you have to take off your shoes as you go through airport security (unless you are cleared through TSA PreCheck), and you're not allowed to have more than 3.4 ounces of liquid in your hand or in your carry-on bag as you enter the boarding area. Was it always this way? Absolutely not!

These restrictions are due to a ripple effect from the terrorist attacks of September 11, 2001—and other plane-related terrorist acts that took place not long after that day. Yet, decades later, we still have rules today that came out of that era! What happened then became the *new normal,* some significant aspects of which are still currently with us.

It's the same with the pandemic that began in 2020. Now that people can finally take off their masks, gather in large groups, and begin traveling again, how is the new normal being defined?

The same applies to tech. Businesses that survived the pandemic were forced to shift from a physical presence to digital, catapulting the success of online video services like Zoom. Zoom's usage exploded during COVID-19, when people were forced to conduct work meetings, academic classes—even children's birthday parties, happy hours, musical performances, and more—remotely!)

Which of the digital trends that started or sped up in the pandemic will continue to be a daily part of our lives for years—or even decades—to come?

Having a personal transformation framework will enable you to reinvent yourself no matter the era or times. It will help you to navigate the next unpredictable wave of digital advances, and it will provide you with a model to accelerate your success even in the midst of uncertain times.

Turning to your framework for making decisions and navigating the choppy waters around you (personally and professionally) will become a normal part of who you are and how you respond to the ups and downs of the transforming world around you.

Questions for Reflection

- How did the 2020 global pandemic affect your life, both personally and professionally?
- What are some ways that you were able to develop resiliency?
- What other personal transformations did you experience because of the pandemic?

FIVE

Is This Book (Right) for You?

I n order to stand out, become more visible, and attract a steady flow of opportunities in this new season, you must be willing to transform, pivot, and reinvent yourself. This starts with a personal framework for change that allows you to focus on a small subset of things, since it's not practical or motivating to focus on all changes at once. Becoming who you were meant to be in the digital world through your unique potential is not a race; it's a journey. Think of it as a marathon that should be paced, planned with a strategy, and executed within bite-sized achievable steps.

Let's take a look at the personal transformation framework— consisting of five principles— that has guided my own pivots and changes to become a unique leader who is set apart in the digital world.

1. Renew your mindset.

To try something new—whether it's changing careers, entering a new market, or transitioning industries—it is important that you first deal with your mindset. Doing so will guide your purpose and your actions. Your actions are how you respond to the conditions and circumstances around you—or not. A changed mindset will help you to change your actions and the way that you respond to shifts in your personal life and career. A transformed mind leads to a renewed sense of purpose, a fresh perspective, and an intrinsic motivation to take risks and learn new things. It's natural for our minds to fill up with self-doubt and focus on negative thinking. According to Dr. Rick Hanson, psychologist and senior fellow at UC Berkeley, our brains are hardwired for negativity—this is known as the negativity bias. In this book, I will share personal approaches I've used to overcome my own "stinking-thinking" to boldly pivot and transform my mindset to BECOME.

2. Discover and unleash your purpose.

Uncovering your purpose in the world is not easy, and it's not always a clear process. To understand the original intent of why you are here on this earth and what you were born to achieve simply are not easy questions to answer. Many people spend their lives reacting to the day-to-day instead of thinking deeply about what truly drives them and their careers. It is important to understand what you were destined to accomplish with your life. I clearly understand that the purpose and vision for my life determines the outcomes for my career . . . and my ultimate destination, and I'll share my process with you.

Because I'm so connected to my purpose, when I stand in a room with others, I am continuously set apart. I'm differentiated from the person standing next to me by the unique gifts I've applied to my career for the greater good, the things I want to achieve to help and empower others. I stand out because of the unique way I've chosen to apply my gifts and skills to fulfill my purpose. I am excited to unpack for you the discovery of purpose and how to unleash it into the world to help business leaders uncover their purpose in the digital economy.

3. Increase your research capacity.

One incredible superpower I have cultivated over the years is perfecting my research skills to increase my knowledge base. I've learned how to use this wisdom to become more influential and deeply connected to others. As the global economy becomes more interconnected across cultures, language, ethnicities, and time zones, my ability to connect and influence across these differences is an important unicorn trait that I believe sets me apart. Making deep connections is not easy. So, I take the time to research an individual's culture so I understand their values and beliefs. I research the market and customers to deeply understand their needs so I can engage in more influential and connected conversations with targeted outcomes. I am always researching to better understand the world around me so that no matter how difficult a conversation becomes, I am able to persevere and find common ground through the universal experiences that connect each of us.

Cultivating effective research techniques is a critical skill that gives me the ability to breathe life into a vision, concept, or business idea through a unique lens developed by absorbing volumes of information, connecting the dots and making data actionable for others. Your ability to cultivate purposeful research skills will provide you with insights that can empower leaders to better understand their company, the position it holds in the market, patterns to improve that position, and guidance to solve complex problem in a way that gives them competitive differentiation. Research gives you a unique lens to recognize patterns and gain fresh perspectives that can be used to discover new market opportunities, products, or services that businesses can bring to market. This valuable skill sets you apart from the pack.

4. Cultivate your intelligences.

Activating a combination of intelligences beyond my IQ has been a game-changing differentiator in my career. Howard Gardner, a famous Harvard psychologist, provided a framework for us to tap into the multiple intelligences that affect how we learn and work in his 1983 book *Frames of Mind*. His theory demonstrates that while an individual maybe particularly strong in one set of abilities such as visual intelligence or analytical intelligence, that person can go beyond a single competency to possess a broad range of intelligences that empowers them to make a greater impact with a combined set of intelligences. In this book, I address Emotional Intelligence (EQ), Creative Intelligence (CQ), and Digital Intelligence (DQ), and I explain how I've used these intelligences together to accelerate my career and differentiate myself. I show how I draw from these intelligences jointly to increase my influence, my ability to solve complex problems, and my talent for discovering fresh ideas that have yet to be imagined. Activating your multiple intelligence provides a pathway to unique success, whether you are an entrepreneur or a digital worker in any industry. Your ability to set yourself apart through your combined intelligences, knowledge, and experiences gives you a unique capacity that takes you far beyond the boundaries that cultivating a single intelligence imposes.

5. Deploy your gifts.

There is a difference between being *employed* and being *deployed*. To be employed means that someone has hired you for work. To be deployed means that you have strategically distributed your gifts for others to use. Once you understand the power of cultivating your gifts so you can deploy them to others at scale, you can multiply the value you bring to their lives. As Albert Einstein once said: "Try not to become a man of success, but rather try to become a man of value." Einstein recognized that our value is directly linked to our success. When we perfect our gifts and abilities, our value grows, as does our capacity to influence others and achieve success in life.

To prosper in the digital world, you need to do more than merely hope for success. You must be intentional about reinventing your mindset, skills, and experiences on a continual basis.

This starts with imagining the future world and your role in it. With the oceans of information and online resources available to you, you are in a great position to shape and influence the future of this world—so that you are leading digital transformation from the front and not falling behind.

Once you can understand and tap into that, you then need to see yourself in that new world. What are you passionate about? What is your dream for yourself in this digital world? Educating and empowering others? Building software programs? Inventing breakthrough work in robotics? Talking to a room of business leaders to help them reimagine future aspects of their companies? Teaching "envisioning" workshops?

Whatever you're passionate about is what you must delve deeply into, because it is limitless. There are roles, opportunities, and occupations that have yet to be invented—and you can be one of the people to fill them. You could also be one of the people creating these new areas. Be bold in being whatever it is you're called to be.

As you go through the process of personal transformation, your goal should be to make sure that the changes you're making are relevant. They must also be purposeful and align to outcomes important to the leaders you plan to guide and influence. Your personal framework will provide the steps and the structure needed get to your end destination.

I have been coaching individuals and groups since 2006 in areas of personal transformation, helping them to effectively transition their careers in rapidly shifting economies so they have the right skills, competencies, and capabilities to move into their new roles.

The goal is that when those I've taught and coached show up for an interview or seek to rapidly advance in hyper-competitive environments, they have a framework to help them stand out; get noticed by decision makers (including those with the power to hire); and attract excellent opportunities—even in the midst of a crowded and competitive market.

The faces and names of those I've helped have rotated and changed since I first started coaching. But what hasn't changed is my guidance. It has remained the same, whether I am speaking with:

- High school students transitioning to their next level in life, whether it be attending college or an alternative learning path, in order to transition into the digital world
- New corporate and non-profit interns who desire to move up the ladder rapidly

- Workers were laid off from long-standing careers and stay-at-home parents who are ready to return to the workforce
- Experienced, high-performing employees who have been overlooked and have hit the glass ceiling

My guidance is the same because I've created a framework built on a solid foundation of proven principles and areas of focus that enable my clients to transcend eras, times, and economic situations.

If you desire to stand out in today's world and achieve unprecedented success, then this book is for you. I look forward to sharing my framework with you and watching you soar, shine, and be sought after—and increase in value—in the digital world.

Questions for Reflection

- What is your intentional plan to improve your research skills in today's digital economy?
- How can you move from merely being *employed by others* to being actively *deployed for others*?
- Using the power of your imagination, how do you see the future world and your place in it?

PART II: FIVE STEPS TO DISCOVER, DEVELOP, AND DEPLOY YOURSELF

This world needs the fresh ideas that are locked inside of you. Today's businesses need new insights and perspectives that only you can unleash.

A truly innovative economy harnesses the contributions of all its citizens, resulting in more ideas of the people and by the people to accelerate performance and the transformation of businesses, governments, and other organizations striving to become digital leaders.

Equally important, the accessibility of innovation to all can yield new ideas for improving living standards, health, and overall well-being, particularly when ideas come from communities directly impacted by problems created by the same people trying to solve them.

Our startup communities require new levels of digital intelligence. We must move beyond the "elite" cluster of digital workers and innovators people think of when they hear the word "tech" by making tech skills and jobs available to everyone. We must build a pipeline of digital-ready innovators who collectively unleash their power to create new levels of social and corporate value and accelerate digital transformation in businesses, governments, non-profits, startups, and other organizations all around the world.

Your ability to reinvent yourself is vital!

We are all at the beginning of this digital journey, and the opportunities are limitless, especially as business leaders are rethinking their roles and expanding the existing skills of their current workforce (known as "upskilling") for their companies to become more competitive.

In a joint research project, the World Economic Forum and the Boston Consulting Group reported that managing skills in the digital age requires organizations to invest in technologies that encourage lifelong learning and skills to increase so they can maximize the value of their investments. For you, this means cultivating new habits and disciplining your activities to acquire more knowledge, wisdom, and intelligence. You want to attract business leaders or customers and become an influential part of their vision and the things they want to achieve in the world.

Your unicorn spirit is needed now more than ever. For today's businesses to thrive in this emerging world, they must go beyond technology to making digital investments for their companies and infuse innovation into every process and capability their company and employees engage in.

You are the heartbeat of the digital world for these companies. So, think, believe, and act like a Digital Unicorn—because that's who you are!

One of the greatest advantages digital companies have is the speed with which they get new innovations to market. Businesses that are moving toward becoming digital-ready also understand the value that unique and differentiated cultures bring to the table. You represent this unique culture. Therefore, shifting your mindset and acquiring a new set of skills should be top of mind for you.

Business leaders understand that creating a digitally intelligent culture is a top way to distinguish them from competitors. They also understand the power of integrating technologies such as artificial intelligence (AI), machine learning (ML), big data, and the Internet of Things (IoT) into the fabric of their core business processes. As you personally transform to deeply learn, understand, adopt, and heavily consume an organization's digital investments, you empower them to surpass the competition and uniquely differentiate themselves in the market.

Most leaders are just beginning to imagine the workplace of the future. No one fully understands how the digital environment will—or should—evolve. One thing that leaders agree on is that they must empower their employees to think differently in terms of the digital innovation possibilities they can imagine. They also must think differently about the experiences they deliver to customers and how to prepare the right response to consumer and marketplace needs. This is the workplace you are reinventing yourself for.

As the walls between different departments and divisions are pulled down, collaboration begins taking place where those boundaries once prevented it from happening. As you tap into the unicorn spirit hidden within you and cultivate skills that will power your success in digital environments, remember that we are all starting on a level playing field when it comes to understanding our unique potential in the digital world.

For example, when I started my Mixed Reality and Immersive Tech learning journey, I knew nothing about 3D technology, HoloLens, or augmented and mixed reality— much less how to integrate concepts like AI and machine learning into 3D technology. I recall reaching out to one of my engineering colleagues engineers and saying: "Hey there, I may need a little support since I'm new to this team. Here are some questions that I'm unclear about." He replied, "Well, give me a little time since I've got do my own research, because all of this is new for me too." We both laughed, and I said, "But you've been working on 3D technology for a long time." He replied, "Yes, but not in terms of integrating AI and machine learning directly into 3D. It's all new stuff that we need to experiment with and learn more about." This blew my mind. It also reminded me that none of us have all the answers—it's OK to be a bit fearful and vulnerable when we're learning something new. We can learn with confidence and have the courage to push beyond the fear that tries to hold us back from exploring new things.

I want you to take risks and learn more about these digital technologies—*despite* your fears. We are all five-year-olds again when it comes to all this new digital stuff. We have to learn together. We have to discover together, and through the journey we're going to take in this book, you'll get a better understanding of your purpose and your gifts, and you'll learn to go deeper to tap into this innovative spirit. It's a really great opportunity to discover what you have inside of you and what big problems you're going to solve through your unique lens and perspective.

We help leaders maximize the return of their digital investments when we show up curious, with a lifelong-learning mindset and tremendous excitement to push beyond using the standard tools to leverage the breadth of the digital investments available to us, thereby increasing our digital capacity and in turn, unleashing our clients' greatest potential.

SIX

Step 1: Reset Your Mindset to See with a New Lens

The beginning of your personal transformation starts with your mindset. You must see in yourself what others don't. Your mind is your thought-center, and it holds the key to your personal transformation. We can define mindset as a lens or mental frame that selectively organizes and translates information, positioning us toward a unique way of understanding an experience, while guiding us toward a subsequent set of actions and responses. That's why it is so important to have a vision for your life. Vision imposes discipline on your actions so that you can get to the end state or destination you've envisioned for yourself. Taking the time to reflect on where you see yourself in the digital world is the start to building great confidence to achieve more for you—and others.

Let's look at three characteristics of a digital mindset:

- **Vision** to see limitless possibilities in the digital world
- **Belief** in the purpose of digital
- **Comfort** with uncertainty in the digital world

Vision to See Limitless Possibilities in the Digital World

At the start of my career as a business architect and consultant, a big focus of my role was spent helping customers to envision their future business so we could map the right software applications to their business needs and requirements. I remember spending lots of time in large conference rooms leading envisioning workshops with executive leaders and taking them through a structured process to define the current state of their business—where they are today—and the future state of their business—where they are going. I drew lots of pictures of concepts on a whiteboard to show the current and future business in real-time, helping these leaders to view their future business visually. We would then map their goals, objectives, and desired outcomes, and then paint a picture of where they saw their business in the next three to five years.

These workshops were designed to get these executive leaders to think, to get them into a mind frame of dreaming, of imagining their future business. We would continue the process by thinking through all problems that could potentially disrupt or negatively interrupt their journey to achieve their goals. We asked all the right questions to help these leaders look at all sides of the business problems identified—even uncovering problems they had yet to encounter. Finally, we would enter a new imagine zone to envision how new technologies and digital investments could solve the problems, and we then imagined new problems that could arise—such as a change in skills required to interact with these new technologies or how the landscape of their business would change. These sessions went beyond dreaming and imagining the next big thing to anticipate all the risks and new challenges that could be imposed, and then think through ways to lessen the impact of these challenges. Then we would start to brainstorm new ideas—real, concrete steps we could take to tackle each of the problems identified.

What we covered in these workshops provided an incredible framework to approach my own personal transformation, starting with the discovery. Where did I see myself in the digital future? What steps could I take to thrive in that future? This process could only be successful if I could imagine, see what's not yet been seen. What did my journey look like to get to my destination in the new digital economy?

Vision is the ability to see the future through a picture in your mind. You're able to see things others don't and imagine a world that doesn't yet exist. With your sight, you can see pictures, but with vision you can *paint* pictures—within your mind. The ability to envision means to imagine that something is likely to happen in the future.

Today, as a strategy and innovation thought leader, my role depends on having a vision and the ability to see what is unseen. This is a critical skill for me, especially when it comes to understanding how digital breakthroughs impact businesses and showing leaders their limitless potential in the digital world, even while there is much uncertainty and ambiguity about the future. It is my job to inspire everyone around me to see a future that is fictional and build the right strategic plans to drive business even though they are unable to visualize concrete outcomes. I'm the one who can see through the fog of uncertainties. My gift is simplifying all the complexities that the future imposes on the imagination; I help leaders connect the dots between where they are today and where they are going.

Four Actions to Help You Vision Your Future

1. **Cultivate your imagination.** You must be able to deep think and ponder different questions concerning what's possible. Place your focus on developing the skills needed to ask the right questions and uncover clues about what

the digital future holds for you. This also connects back to your purpose: Why are you here? What are you meant to achieve? Look at your mobile device. What business can you launch through your phone? How do you move from being just a consumer to a business owner using the same mobile phone? Look at the materials around you— your car, your truck. Do you see a mobile delivery business? What about your workplace? Are there things you complain about yet haven't been able to come up with any solutions? Unicorns see what others don't. Learn to cultivate the skill of asking questions. Practice deep thinking so you push your imagination beyond its normal limitations.

2. **Look around to study the needs of others.** Specifically, study your customers and the people you serve within your communities. Begin to question and see things from as many dimensions and angles as possible. Be an empathetic and actionable observer. Search for the root or motivation of a problem so that you can imagine solutions that solve challenges from the source—the origin. To see the digital future, you must develop the ability to zoom in and zoom out with a new lens—a fresh perspective—and see what's on the other side of the problem. Become skilled at going beyond the surface and seeing all sides of an issue. Then learn to narrow what you have discovered to start shaping and framing the problem; this requires applying "why" and "how" questioning techniques to each problem component. From there, you can uncover actionable opportunities.

3. **Build the right connections to think with others—in teams.** You should thirst to be around other visionaries and creatives, so you can share your ideas, exchange

perspectives, collaborate, and come out on the other end with potentially stronger and more interesting ideas than you could ever generate alone. Getting insight into how other group members envision what's next on the digital horizon allows you to discover new answers from different lenses. What you're learning from everyone around you helps generate the best ideas and innovations, and you're building up the synergy that collective brainstorming creates. As you problem solve and uncover next-level ideas, along with the combined insights and viewpoints you've gathered from others, you begin to see a bigger picture of what the digital future looks like. You have the power and ingenuity as a unicorn to open the door to new approaches to collective thinking and creativity. You introduce others to new, collaborative ways that build perspective on challenges and bring together creative ideas interactively with a collective crowd.

4. **Integrate and connect the dots.** In his ground-breaking work *The New Economics*, W. Edwards Deming states: "It would be better if everyone would work together as a system, with the aim for everybody to win. What we need is cooperation and transformation to a new style of management." I have spent two decades of my career collaborating and integrating the perspectives of others, so I understand the power and importance of working alongside others to produce winning outcomes. However, receiving ideas within a collective is just the start. The key is to translate the shared perspectives into actionable gains, integrating multiple viewpoints into your ideas and connecting the dots—which means to bring together information from

different places in order to understand something as a whole or how different things affect each other. This act of integrating ideas allows you to connect your thoughts, research, and outside thinking, and then activate and apply the synergy that comes from doing so. Remember, you have the power to become a digital visionary!

Belief in the Purpose of Digital

Mahatma Gandhi once said, "Your beliefs become your thoughts, your thoughts become your words, your words become your actions, your actions become your habits, your habits become your values, your values become your destiny." To have belief in something simply means that you agree in your mind that something is true and believe in its existence. You accept that something is actual, factual, and true. You must have this level of belief about your digital abilities and skills, about your capacity to learn at the speed of change in the digital world. You believe in the limitless possibilities you can achieve in this digital economy.

With this belief, you are committed to become someone who will use digital for good, you're going to leverage all of the digital skills in this area to develop and empower the world around you. Waking up in the morning and having that level of belief is critical as you continue your learning journey. In believing and walking in your purpose, you are here not only to empower business leaders to unleash their full digital potential, but to do the same within your home and community. The question isn't what can you achieve in the digital world if you believe in your capabilities, but what can you *not* achieve?

You have to look within, especially in this season when there are so many forces around you telling you what you can't do. The digital world is limitless, so look within and say to yourself: "Everything is possible in this new era. There is nothing I can't achieve." As we've learned, the key is getting out of your comfort zone and doing something new every day—or at least once a week. Take small steps and do something you haven't done before. For example, I decided that I wanted real-world experience with the Internet of Things—IoT for short. IoT is about taking all the things in the world and connecting them to the internet. Although I understood the theory behind IoT and the concepts from an architecture perspective, I had never built anything tangible, like a product or an app. I could stand in front of large crowds or executive decision makers and deliver highly influential talks about IoT and the value to their business; however, it bothered me that I had never actually coded or configured an IoT application or device.

I remained curious and growth-minded. I took the risk of ordering my first IoT kit on the Amazon website. I ordered my first Raspberry Pi IoT Kit; this would allow me to set up my own sensors at home and be able to turn my lights on and off through my phone. How cool was that! Then the fear set in—fear that I was a terrible programmer. Fear that I would fail. Every negative thought you could imagine came raging through my mind. However, I know how to speak to myself when feelings of doubt and fear arise. So I simply reoriented my mindset and asked myself: "What's the worst that can happen? That I push a button, and something doesn't work?" I had to get over the fear of connecting IoT devices in my own home so I could achieve more for others.

A present-day example: My grandmother, who is eighty-seven, wants to live independently with some help from hired caretakers and not be put in a nursing home. I reached out to a startup company in Atlanta with a cool idea to create a smart connected home for independent living, which I felt was a game-changing concept for elderly since the majority would rather live at home than in nursing home facilities. I envisioned connecting sensors to her refrigerator, coffeepot, and other devices attached to motion-detecting cameras. All the data then would be uploaded to the cloud, where I would be able to monitor her throughout the day via a mobile app that sends notifications and alerts when strange events occurred. So now, as an aging individual, she can have independent living. I don't have to put her in a nursing home. This is the power of believing in yourself. Your strong, unwavering belief in your ability to achieve greatness in this digital era must overpower any fears you have about your success.

If you're like me and landed your very first job in a restaurant, your have an incredible opportunity to learn and innovate within your mind. Instead of simply showing up to take orders, wait tables, clean tables, or work the grill— imagine expanding your mindset to innovate on the next big thing . . . right where you are. For example, as you are in the moment doing your job by serving your customers, take a step back to understand each process it takes to deliver the best experience to your customers. Evaluate every step from greeting customers upon arrival and seating the customers to taking their order and delivering their order—all of the processes it takes to delight each customer. Then, as you develop a perspective, consider ways you would introduce more automation and digitization into the current experience. This is where transformation for businesses begins— within our own thoughts and imagination. Your belief about who you are and what you can accomplish must connect to the vision you have for your life and for others. So wherever you decide to start your career journey and throughout the evolution of your career, always seek to improve the world around you, while planning your exit strategy and entrance into your digital future at the same time.

Comfort with Uncertainty in the Digital World

The 2020 pandemic unleashed new levels of ambiguity and uncertainty that many had to learn to navigate. The term *uncertainty* refers to situations that involve unknown information. Uncertainty occurs when the circumstances we are familiar with take a turn, seemingly right before our eyes, shifting from a stable situation to an unstable one. Now no one knows what will happen next or how things will unfold, or what a "new normal" will look like when things settle.

Our brains are wired to assess potential threats, and our nervous system goes into high alert when faced with uncertainty and ambiguity—it's the fight-or-flight syndrome within each of us. Dr. Dino Signore, a business psychologist for entrepreneurial education, has developed steps to navigate uncertainty using neuroscience. His work helps us to understand that we are not meant to become victims of the things we don't understand or the uncertainties we encounter.

Instead, what serves us best is to surrender and simply let go of things we absolutely cannot control and instead focus on the things we actually can control. It's a productive perspective that can help us to feel balanced and centered—even in the midst of the unknown. The digital world presents uncertainties in every area, from the technologies we use every day to the way digital has impacted who we are. In difficult times we must resist the impulse to become unstable ourselves; we must choose to evolve and become more resilient, able to withstand all the uncertain forces around us.

Let's walk through four actions that can help you deal with uncertain or ambiguous situations—and be successful in your journey to become digital.

1. *Write out your thoughts.* In your journal, write down all your fears and negative thoughts. You can't fix what you can't see—and you must see all the negative things that you fear and unable to comprehend. Writing out your thoughts will help you clear your mind. Put down the things that worry you—uncertainties, emotions, feelings. Write about what you're thinking, what you're fearful of. The great thing is that once you've written all these things down, you've freed them from your head and your heart, releasing a new mental capacity that paves the way for positive thinking to enter your mind and overcome each negative or fearful thought.

2. *Remain focused on your destination.* I've learned that the best thing I can do for myself in times of uncertainty is to stay on task and keep the vision for my future in immediate focus so I overcome my fear and anxiety with a clear picture

of my end goals. What is my secret to staying focused? Well, as soon as uncertainty begins to reveal itself, I re-evaluate my purpose, vision, and goals. I also revisit my priorities that are in place to help me get me to my destination and remain disciplined on the activities that will drive the outcomes I've envisioned for my future. With this focused mindset, I'm able to reclaim control by asking many questions, such as:

- What do these uncertain times represent?
- What new habits or behaviors do I need to develop in order to achieve my goal?
- What's blocking me from being able to make the changes that I need to make?
- Do I have the right training?
- Am I on course?
- What needs to shift in order to accelerate my goals during these uncertain times?

By answering these questions boldly and confidently, you can replace the fear that comes with uncertainty.

3. *Flood your mind with positive thinking.* During times of uncertainty, I've learned how not to make fear and anxiety the loudest voices in my mind. To do this, there are a few things I practice daily. First I am committed to start each day with positivity. When the day starts out, I begin it with positive, happy music or meditation, or by writing positive affirmations on sticky notes that I place on the bathroom mirror to lift my mood as I get ready for the day.

Second, I practice positive self-talk, which is the most effective thing in my life to interrupt negative thinking. I start this process by removing negative words from my vocabulary, and I refrain from saying negative things to myself. I'm gentle with my words and highly encouraging.

When negative thoughts enter my mind, I quickly (and loudly) interrupt the negativity and speak positive things into the atmosphere. Go ahead. Try it now.

Finally, I surround myself with positive thinkers. With social media and virtual video, I'm able to unlock positivity in my life anytime uncertainties begin to overwhelm me. Whether it's through text, messenger, or video chats, I can crowdsource positive thinking anytime—meaning I can source positive words from open online groups and create a chain of positive affirmations from my circle of friends.

4. *Calm your emotions through being at peace.* One of the greatest strengths I have cultivated over the years is the ability to stay calm in the midst of uncertain times. It's not easy to control our emotions when confronted with the intense situations or circumstances in which there are truly no answers. Exercising self-control is a habit that we must put into practice each day. As one of the best known Latin writers, Publilius Syrus, puts it, "Anyone can hold the helm when the sea is calm." In other words, it's easy to remain calm when things are going well. The true test in life is how you respond when trouble arises. What kind of human being do you become? One who is unstable? Worried? Angry? Scared? Do you crack under pressure or remain level-headed, calm, and peaceful? There is value

in the ability to hold things steady and persevere through difficult and challenging times when everyone else seems to be falling apart.

I enjoy the fact that other people can count on me to bring peace to fearful, ambiguous situations. However, this takes practice. It also takes a deeper level of honesty and vulnerability to be able to share with others where things may not be working or have the guts to boldly communicate (with empathy) where things are failing. The key lies within the inherent ability to see a picture of the future and have the emotional discipline to stay focused and believe that you will reach your destination despite the uncertain times and ambiguous situations.

Retrain Your Brain

I continuously retrain my brain. I find that whenever my mind repeatedly tells me that I cannot achieve something, and I actually believe it, it is very difficult for me to innovate. It's impossible to be in creative spaces mentally when I've given up on my ability to actually be effective and have breakthroughs.

The digital world requires something unique and different from each of us. It requires us to tap into something much greater than what our own minds think we can achieve. Resetting and retraining our brain to think positively and imagine beyond what we can currently see is critical to having a digital mindset. Let's go over the steps involved in retraining your thinking so you can visualize yourself as a high performer in the digital realm.

1. ***Start a personal reflection list.*** Identify everything that is
    mentally preventing you from seeing the greatness within
    yourself. You can write your thoughts in a paper notebook,
    or you can write them digitally. I use a mobile Notes App
    to deeply reflect and be authentic about what I'm saying
    about myself. I ask myself the following questions:

    - What am I fearful of?
    - Where do I lack the courage to think differently to take
      on new habits?
    - Why do I do think the same way all the time?
    - What's stopping me from making a change in this area?
    - How do I get started?

    So, step one is an honest assessment of the things that
    prevent you from seeing the best in yourself and being of
    value to the digital world. It's like an excavation process
    to dig up old, negative things below the surface that are
    holding me back.

    Reframe all of your negative thinking. Instead of saying,
    "This will never work," or "You're not good enough," or
    "You don't have enough knowledge," or "You're not smart
    enough," reframe all that by reflecting deeply on the things
    you've accomplished, things you know you're great at. This
    new list will act as a counterweight to your ongoing list
    of negative thoughts. For example, when your mind tells
    you something will not work, you say instead, "This will
    work, and if I run into challenges, I will learn from the
    experience and make it better."

Even if you spend just fifteen minutes per day capturing and writing down every thought that comes to mind, this will help you study the patterns of your thinking.

Choose a mantra for each day—or perhaps choose one you will repeat to yourself for an entire season—for instance, all winter. To get you started, here are some examples of ones I've repeated to myself out loud when I'm home alone, and internally when I'm struggling in public places and need motivation:

- "Today, will be a phenomenal day."
- "I will move to the next level as a digital thought leader."
- "I will learn, achieve, and accomplish more, so that I can empower all of those around me to become responsibly digital, by choosing their digital platforms and devices— and how they spend their time on them—wisely."

It's important to have a mantra that keeps you motivated, so that when someone or something tries to introduce negative thinking into your space, you can talk it down and out of your pathway. That way, negative situations can't prevent you from reaching your intended destination. Address the things that are physically around you that are preventing you from progressing in your thinking. Develop relationships with positive people and spend more time with them. This is extremely important. Personally, I have a small handful of people that I interact with on a personal basis outside of work. We encourage and motivate one another via weekly motivational text messages that reinforce upbeat, optimistic thinking. I surround myself with fellow digital innovators because it is extremely difficult to innovate when my mind is burdened with negativity. The heavy mental load that negativity breeds is too big for innovation to unleash itself under that weight.

Changing your surroundings, clearing negative thoughts, and resetting your mind will make room for you to focus on your positive destination. In order for you to be able to achieve all you've set out to achieve in the digital world, it is extremely important for your mind to connect with your habits, and your behaviors with your actions—which all lead to your ability to become purposefully digital.

2. *Move beyond your comfort zone.* Everything around you will continue to change, whether you decide to change yourself or not. The only thing that separates those who are successful in the digital world from those who don't realize success is the willingness to take action—even when things are unclear and uncertain.

In fact, digital high performers seek new businesses or jobs that are vague and uncertain so they can shape the future of these roles with their own thinking and vision. Personally, this is my sweet spot. But I had to cultivate this thinking and learn to take risks, even when I was uncom- fortable and didn't know the outcomes. An exponential mindset is all about trying new things and thinking differ- ently in the midst of uncertainty.

Discovering ways to take a leap, learn, and grow—and then repeating that process over and over—is key to your success in the digital era. It's important to increase your knowledge, awareness, actions, and achievements, and be able to do this over time and more rapidly than others in your field.

3. *Try something new that you haven't done yet.* Trying
   something new will help you leap to exponential thinking.
   For example, I've never written a book before, so this is
   my big leap. My desire to write a story that will guide and
   inspire others to go through their own personal transformations has forced me outside of my comfort zone.
     How did I write this book? I took it step by step, day by
   day. I extended deadlines when necessary to get chapters
   done, and I became very flexible. It took a lot of research
   and so much learning to be able to develop a growth mindset and then share these insights with the rest of the world.
   Once you've completed or accomplished your first new
   thing, then try your second new thing, and then your third.
     Practice trying something new over and over again—and
   make that part of your daily your habit.

Questions for Reflection

- If journaling isn't already one of your habits, what steps
  can you take to start keeping a personal reflection list,
  challenging yourself to address your fears, habits, and
  thinking and then reframe them?
- What are one or two things you can do to move out of
  your comfort zone—intentionally?
- What is something new that you've never done but are
  willing to try?

SEVEN

Step 2: Discover and Unleash Your Purpose

S teve Jobs said, "Being the richest man in the cemetery doesn't matter to me. Going to bed at night saying we've done something wonderful, that's what matters to me." Purpose is your secret sauce.

Purpose separates you from the pack.

Imagine you are in a room with twenty people who do the exact same job as you. What sets you apart? What makes you a unique standout? Now, imagine you are in a meeting with these twenty people, speaking with a business leader. Whom do you think will make the most memorable impression—especially when everyone in the room does the same thing? The person with purpose. Purpose will give you additional dimensions— greater depth—and unleash hidden layers of your character; this will set you apart from the crowd.

Purpose is your aim, mission, intention, target, and end destination. Purpose guides your decisions in life. It shapes your goals, objectives, and outcomes. Purpose influences behavior. It gives meaning and a sense of direction. In the digital world, purpose is about being able to feel grounded in why you exist during this particular time in history.

What do you want to accomplish in the digital era? What will be your legacy? Every time I discuss this topic during my coaching sessions, people always ask, "Why is it important to understand my individual purpose? Why should I even care?" I get why someone may think he or she doesn't need a purpose in order to be successful in life. But I know that for me, being grounded and understanding why I am here is essential.

Having a purpose when I walk into a room gives me a level of confidence—even when I'm faced with uncertainty.

I find that when I am not grounded in my mission, then I waste time. I don't want to waste my time or anyone else's time. My unique purpose is inextricably linked to the activities that I focus on daily. Why would I participate in an unproductive activity that doesn't connect back to my purpose? That's not to say you can't rest or have downtime. However, when you are active, purpose helps you be selective and make the most of your time.

A global study showed that over 80 percent of executives believe that a strong sense of purpose among employees and those in leadership affects an organization's ability to transform and thrive in a competitive world.

These business leaders are aware that they must connect their organizational vision and objectives to their employees' work so that employees have a sense of purpose. For me the question always is: How can I help business leaders, entrepreneurs, and nonprofits fully realize their purpose in their market or communities if I have never taken the time to realize my own?

Why I'm here is clear to me: My purpose in the digital world is to leverage technologies, platforms, and solutions to enhance the lives of others and to make their lives better. I believe that the inventions, creations, or ideas I have will help to build and create a better planet. I'm very clear why I exist during this particular time in history.

My purpose drives the plan for my life. My purpose drives the roadmap for my learning, knowledge, and training. My purpose drives my habits. It's more than just connecting understanding my purpose, however; I must activate and deploy it. Purpose also helps me to think holistically about my entire people ecosystem. What am I doing to help my mother and grandmother to have great, independent lives as they grow older? What am I doing for my nephew and niece to make sure they are responsible when they use digital technologies? How am I helping my neighbors, my community, and nonprofit organizations so that I empower young people every day to discover their purpose in this digital era? The more I learn and understand these digital capabilities, the more I tap into my own personal transformation and go deeper into my own purpose.

Understand that your skill set is only the beginning. The fact that you have knowledge across a span of technologies is awesome. But how are you activating those capabilities to drive purpose in your own life and in the lives of others? What do you intend to do with all the rich knowledge and capabilities you're using to build your talents? How will you *fully* manifest your role as a proactive Digital Citizen?

Why are you here? You're not here just to suck up air and take resources. You're here to breathe life into things—because you have been given an opportunity to do so. But it's OK to start the process by admitting, "I don't know. I've never really thought about what I was born to be—and do."

Four Actions to Discover Your Purpose

Reintroduce Yourself to You

Introspection is a powerful tool we can tap into to examine our own mental and emotional processes. Of course you've known yourself your entire life; however, if you don't pause to deeply reflect on the areas of your life that are shifting, drastically changing, impacted by the current year's events, or slowly dying due to lack of care, then it will be challenging for you to know if you're on track to meet your goals or if you're completely off target, wandering aimlessly where the wind blows.

Many of our habits, behaviors, and actions are already programmed within our subconscious. We follow the same routine patterns each day. We get up. Shower. Brush our teeth. Eat breakfast. Check in with social media. Go to school or work (unless you're schooled or work from home). Eat lunch. Sign off from school or work. Eat dinner. Socialize. Go to bed. And if there are kids involved, these activities double. The point is, it's easy for us to become so familiar with ourselves and so absorbed in daily habits that we take a lot of things about ourselves for granted.

The process of annual introspection can be quite revealing. Introspection is simply understanding your strengths and weakness, your potential, how you react to others, or how you respond to situations and environments. The results of this process allow us to deprogram the habits and patterns engrained within our subconscious—the part of the mind we are not fully aware of, yet which influences our actions and emotions.

I create the space and time to go into deep self-reflection with myself, to examine where I am today with my goals. I write down my thoughts about the digital age and my potential. I discuss my thoughts and feelings about what I want to achieve in this era, and assess whether or not I'm on track with my goals. I ask myself, "What are my thoughts and feelings about the digital era? What aspects of my journey do I need to pivot in order to be successful in the digital world?" My focus is not just on uncovering my purpose in life; I also focus on seeing myself in the digital economy and making the impact I want to make.

I self-reflect frequently. Taking the time to become more self-aware allows me to take a step back and get a fresh perspective on what's important to me. How do I view my impact within the digital world? My answer to this determines my activities and my path forward. Self-reflection allows me to better understand the changes that I need to make so I can be more effective helping companies to become their digital selves and uncover their digital purpose.

Start by deep thinking. You may want to help the homeless. I don't want to see child abuse in the world. Personally, I know that's why I'm here. I'm here to create positive change in the world using the technologies available to us. I'm here to change the lives of others, so that they have an opportunity to live their best life on this earth. You want to get clear on your purpose and go even deeper to understand your existence and why you are here?

The more deeply I know myself, the more I become even more authentic, and that helps others to trust me with their vision and critical areas of their business.

Identify Your Unique Abilities

Throughout my career, I've found that the more that I've cultivated my gifts—the greater my career excels. The key to winning during these rapidly changing times is to align with the true nature of who you are at your core—and deeply understand your unique abilities. I interact with so many people every day who are unhappy with their career paths, who are unclear about how they will achieve success in this season of their lives, who don't know how they can become more competitive, or who simply have given up and continue to remain in the same job year after year.

Now imagine if these same people collectively activated their unique gifts within their businesses and communities—and inspired everyone around them to do the same. The world benefits in incredible ways when we discover and deploy our gifts. You begin by simply asking questions and connecting to your true nature. What things are you naturally attracted to? What things do you easily gravitate toward? What are your greatest skills? What ignites your excitement when you're in that moment? What were you born to achieve in this historical time? These questions will get you closer to understanding who you are in this digital world and what your passions are.

When we suppress our natural innate skills, gifts, and talents, unlocking these abilities can be a bit fearful. However, discovering the great unique gifts you have inside truly empowers you to thrive during these rapidly changing times. If you don't take the time to discover your gifts, discover your skills, and be committed to discovering the skills that have yet to be cultivated, it will be fairly challenging to find fulfillment in your career—and even in your life. You must unleash the unique qualities and talents into the world so that businesses, leaders, and communities get the most from you. The world is waiting for you to deploy your gifts to places you have yet to imagine. Your talents, your skills, your experiences, and your unique abilities are needed so others can be empowered to achieve their limitless potential in the digital world.

Become More Curious About You

Valuable things in our minds get buried when we don't cultivate our intellectual curiosity. Going deep within ourselves
to ask smart questions is the gift that we can keep on giving
ourselves every day. Curiosity is a beaming light that guides
the way to our end destination—our purpose. Curiosity keeps
us searching, keeps us discovering, until the valuable things
within our minds are uncovered so they can be cultivated. Peter
Drucker, the renowned management consultant and author, led
his consulting engagements with customers by asking lots of
questions. This is what differentiated his consulting approach
from the other consultants and what still makes him famous
today. His ability to ask intelligent questions through a deeply
curious nature is what set his firm apart. Curiosity is an incredible skill that we must continue to develop throughout our
lives. Curiosity helps us to learn. It helps us grow. It helps us
remember complex things. And it helps us to engage the world
around us in highly differentiated and unique ways.

To become curious there are a few things that are top of
mind. One, I understand the importance of finding the
things that fascinate me, especially about myself. I take
myself through a personal exploration process. I continue
asking questions about the things that light up my spirit
when I'm engaging. What is something I love to do even
when I don't have the time? What do I believe is possible
for my own life? What have I done in my life that I'm most
proud of? If I had one final thing to achieve on this earth
on during my time here, what would I want to achieve?
What legacy do I want to leave? So being curious enables

you to develop the skills to be intellectually curious about the world. Businesses, customers, partners, and others you will tremendously benefit from the gifts you have to offer discovered, developed—and deployed.

Define the Impact You Want to Make in the Digital World

Digital Unicorns are purpose-driven gift cultivators who frequently ask themselves, "How can I create positive change in the world and have an amazing time doing it?" The answer to this question for me is to take small actions every day to show up as an ally for others. It is impossible for me to lead others to their own purpose and gifting if I have yet to discover and cultivate my own. Take the time to consider how you can use your purpose and your gifts to leave a lifelong impact on the world. What issues do you care most about? What issues do the people in your community care most about? What's top of mind for businesses as they approach the digital terrain? How can you show up to help them achieve their mission?

Although you may not be able to fix all the problems of this world, you can make positive contributions. So, get deeply curious and begin to explore the impact you want to make in this world; start with small steps. Today, the world needs bold, confident, innovative thinkers like you to help solve the big challenges we face in our diverse global economy, communities, business environments, and social surroundings. In the famous words of Mahatma Gandhi, "Be the change you wish to see in the world."

Questions for Reflection

- Set aside some time for self-reflection introspection. What do you want to think deeply about?
- What one thing do you most want to accomplish before your time on earth is up?
- What positive impact can you see yourself making in the digital world?

EIGHT

Step 3: Increase Your Research Capacity

You can stay ahead and lead change, or you can ignore change and get left behind.

Today's leaders are looking for those who can exhibit a range of next-level skills that will accelerate their success in this ever-shifting market. This includes the ability to gather and assimilate information in real time from many sources and translate this research into actionable breakthrough strategies that leaders can act on.

Research is one of the top skills that has been critical to advancing my career over the past couple of decades. Research is simply the ability to solve problems or find answers to questions by discovering, analyzing, interpreting, and translating information gathered. Cultivating your research skills will enable you to stay ahead in an adaptive economy.

Business leaders need intelligent workers who can provide market research that enables them to better understand their competitors' strengths and weaknesses, examine their products and translate this into compete strategies, gain customer knowledge so they can get to know their customers more deeply—all in an effort to influence the problems they want to solve and the direction of their business.

Through your unique lens and the skills you have cultivated to process information in real-time and translate into actionable strategies for businesses, startups, and/or community leaders, you can help leaders understand the world around them, which pitfalls to avoid—and which ideas to capitalize on quickly.

Understand the Trends

You can start your research journey by understanding what's happening in the world around you—in terms of the latest technologies, industry trends, and megatrends (including macro and micro-trends).

Tech Trends

As technology continues to change at a rapid pace, it can seem overwhelming to keep up with the tech trends—especially with millions of blogs, websites, and social media sites announcing new tech on a daily basis. Your ability to stay on top of tech trends gives you a competitive advantage in your career and enables you to see and understand the business and tech landscape with a fresh lens. My favorite sites for technology trends are Gartner, Forrester, TechCrunch, The Next Web, Wired, and Digital Trends. Once you discover the tech research that works for you, subscribe to the mailing list and newsletters; these are very informative when seeking the latest updates and newest developments.

Industry Trends

The next type of research I perform focuses on industry trends. An industry trend is a direction or pattern businesses in a specific sector are following or are inclined to move toward. Industry trends have significant impact on business profitability, people, culture, and global markets. These trends predict where an industry is heading, while helping us to understand the present moment. Learning how to interpret this data will help you determine when an opportunity in your career is a good move and when to pivot—change the direction you are heading so that you can better align to your career goals even when markets begin to shift. Industry trend information provides the data, statistics, analysis, references, and considerations required for you to keep your pulse on the market so you are constantly feeding into your personal transformation framework and adjusting your career strategies accordingly. My favorite websites for industry trends are Forrester, GreenBook, Fortune Business Insights, the Big 3 (McKinsey, BCG, and Bain), and Big 4 firms (Deloitte, E&Y, PwC, and KPMG), along with Accenture and Nielsen Market Trends.

Megatrends

The final core research that I perform weekly is around megatrends, including micro and macro trends. Megatrends are long-term structural shifts that influence all aspects of our lives and have permanent consequences for the world around us. Examples of these events include climate change, demographic change, advances in technology—such as autonomous cars or AI—and social change. Megatrends impact business direction, processes, activities, and perceptions about the future. So, as you are growing your knowledge base, it's important to understand where things are going and how these events will impact your career—and your life. Macro-trends are the children of megatrends. While megatrends cover large areas such as advances in technology, macro-trends focus on narrow parts such as Artificial Intelligence, Machine Learning, or Robotics. You can analyze macro-trends by targeting specific demograph ics, types of business, regions, or industries. Understanding macro-forces in the digital economy help you to lead meaningful conversations and stand out from the crowd. This is where I rely on white papers, blogs, and online articles from firms like Deloitte, Accenture, McKinsey, and PwC to explain macro-trend patterns and connect the dots to show how these forces come together to create more value for businesses and offer new ways to deliver experiences to customers. Your ability to lead these kinds of conversations gives you a seat at the table with leaders who are seeking differentiated ways to gain a competitive advantage in the marketplace.

Finally, micro-trends are even more narrowly focused; they are considered the children of macro-trends. These business and economic trends are related to specific industries. They have an indirect impact on the economy versus a direct impact as megatrends and macro-trends do. During the 2020 pandemic, a microtrend that we all witnessed occurring in real time was the thousands of highly educated workers who were suddenly laid off and unsure if their jobs would return due to advances in tech like automation. As a result, we are seeing an increase in new business startups and Gig workers—independent contractors, online platform workers, or temporary workers such as Uber and Amazon drivers who are getting paid for working on multiple short-term projects.

How to Improve Your Research Skills

Sharpening your research skills gives you an edge to quickly find answers to questions or solve complex problems. The fastest way to cultivate your research skills is through online search engines such as Google, Yahoo, Bing, and Ask.com. Through proprietary algorithms—mathematical formulas that are used to determine and display the relevant information from web pages—search engines are a powerful way to quickly understand the latest tech and industry trends. This will allow you to set yourself apart through your vast knowledge set. Research can help you to understand the economic factors impacting the digital world, as well as the greatest technological challenges facing businesses today.

Research also allows you to uncover new digital platforms and systems that businesses can explore and implement to help them accelerate. Connecting the dots is one of the key skills that has allowed me to lead leaders in this digital era. This involves bringing together information from different places and creating a complete picture from those dots or pieces. It also means bringing various facts and ideas together, in order to create a whole picture and a complete understanding.

For example, if you want to learn more about a business or customer, you can collect data from social media conversations on Facebook, LinkedIn, Twitter, and Instagram. Research can be collected by following different procedures, such as creating discussion boards or joining various discussion groups to observe conversational interactions.

Not only do I spend time on social media sites to understand what's happening across industries, I also execute information discovery on search engines on a daily basis. Google and Bing are my go-to's. To be effective with my research on these search engines, I employ different techniques—such as "AND-targeting," which reduces the number of search results returned so you get the data you want to see. For example, if I want to understand the future in digital focused on a particular industry for a specific mega- or macro-factor, I would enter the following search terms: "future digital and retail industry and post-pandemic 2020." This method will return results that provide business and market insights for a given industry focused on perspectives that show the future in digital after the pandemic that started in the year 2020. I spend time reading the most reputable articles. In fact, this search returned a white paper from McKinsey that discussed how to adapt to the new normal in the retail industry after the pandemic.

Another search you can try is the "exact phrase" technique. With this technique, you restrict your search results to the exact word or phrase that describes the information you want to discover. In the search bar, enter your word or phrase in quotation marks. For example, enter "future digital economy." The first search return displayed with this exact phrase is a white paper from the World Economic Forum, which is another one of my favorite websites to get the most relevant research in business, politics, academia, and global economics. The white paper from this search return focused on shaping the future of digital economy and new value creation, which provided relevant insights on how companies should think about new digitally enabled business models post-pandemic.

A final favorite search technique is the "exact file type." This search allows me to limit results to a specific file type—a Word, PowerPoint, or PDF document. I use this technique when I want to read white papers or research papers for a specific topic. Let's continue with the digital micro-trend by using an example search for future digital files. Within the search bar I entered "future digital trends:pdf." The top search return provided a series of PDF files relevant to the future digital trends topic.

A PDF white paper from Accenture surfaced to the top of the search results; it focused on post-digital people leading in a digital world, and how businesses are rethinking the way an enterprise works and redefining the intersection between people and technology.

These are the kinds of insights that empower me to have compelling conversations with business leaders or entrepreneurs who want to better understand how they can differentiate themselves in a digital world.

Stay Current with Technology and Trends

One of the simplest things you can do to better recognize trends is to read research reports or solution guides. Industry leaders often perform original research and compile their findings in one large report, and by taking the time to actually read through it beyond the executive summary, you can almost always find something in it that's valuable and relevant to what's trending right now in your space.

As a thought leader in the technology industry, I follow many industry reports to stay on top of trends—whether it's Gartner's top strategic tech trends, Forrester's emerging technology research reports, or specific research reports from the World Economic Forum report library.

You will discover that as you continue building your knowledge base, you'll soon be recognized as the go-to person for topics about which you have a unique perspective. People will seek you out for your expertise, knowledge, and wisdom. Your reputation as a unicorn thought leader with unique market perspectives will continue to attract others and create an incredible brand for you. This is how you set yourself apart in a crowded market—you get greater understanding and a fresh perspective that no one else sees but you.

Each year, I actually get excited waiting to see what Gartner will unveil within their Top 10 Strategic Technology Trends so I can understand the digital trends that will impact, transform, and shape industries. It's important to keep your pulse on the market, so you can future-proof yourself and remain relevant in rapidly changing times.

As the digital world continues to transform, you must find ways to habitually reinvent yourself. However, it's very challenging to reinvent yourself if you don't deeply research and understand the trends and digital disruptions of the future.

Your purpose and where you are heading, furthered by your skill at connecting the dots as an expert researcher and your ability to understand the times and trends of the future, will become your source of strength. These are competitive advantages and what distinguishes you from others—and separates you from the pack.

For example, I wanted to know the top trends in AI, so I went to my Bing search engine, and typed in "What are the top trends in AI for this year." The search results returned trends showing how AI is becoming increasingly important to the business and consumer worlds and how we are more digitally connected now than ever before. I then went deeper and read each of the blogs, white papers, and research papers to further differentiate myself. This gave me a supreme wisdom to share with others and enabled me to become increasingly influential in the market.

With access to online sites like Forbes and IDC research, there's so much available regarding forward-focused digital trends. Here are four smart steps you can take to make research a cornerstone of your daily life.

1. **Begin with an outline of questions by topic in the areas you want to learn more about.** An outline helps guide your research. Your outline should include a plan for the areas you want to research and the impact you want to make with this new knowledge. For example, I wanted to understand how businesses and entrepreneurs see themselves recovering after the 2020 pandemic and how the "now" normal, new normal, and future normal was shaping up across industries. The outcome of this research would help me to have credible, purposeful, and meaningful conversations with various leaders across industries, with customers, and with my network of sponsors and mentors. I have always enjoyed bringing new perspectives to conversations—unique viewpoints that are credible and well-formed. I understand the impact of empowering others with fresh ideas and new views that they wouldn't have thought of unless I showed up to share my perspective. Make it a habit to go to Bing, Google, or your favorite search engine daily. Tell yourself: "I'm going make it a habit to learn one new thing a day." When you use the internet for research, most search engines allow you to use advanced search preferences to customize your search results. These search techniques will help you find the information you are looking for from credible sources more efficiently.

One of the best ways to develop any new or existing skill is to put it into practice. You can practice developing purposeful research skills by creating small projects for yourself to work on that can help you with a current industry topic or a relevant business event. For example, if you are planning a career pivot, you can practice researching different keyword phrases such as "strategies to make a career pivot" or "how to pivot my career while still working on a current job'. Document the highlights of your learning and leverage the input to create your own personal career pivot framework.

2. **Develop a point of view (PoV).** Once you've completed the research on a given topic, cultivate your own unique perspective based on everything you've learned. Translate your viewpoint into a social blog or LinkedIn post so your thought leadership is on full display. Your goal is to get feedback and input from others around you who have insights and perspectives on that topic, then integrate the shared viewpoints into your personal transformation plan.

3. **Take a risk.** Go beyond blog posts and create a presentation for a business, industry, or social community. Search for upcoming speaking events through the keyword search "call for papers" and add the year you want to see results for. This will bring up speaking events that are seeking speakers. You can also record your viewpoints through a short digital masterclass video and share it directly with your personal networks or on social media sites like LinkedIn and Facebook. You want to take action, sharing and discussing your point of view based on what you've researched and

learned. As you verbalize what you've learned and spread the word, you'll gain a new network of supporters, potential sponsors, and mentors.

4. **Follow publications and influencers in your specific industry or across multiple industries.** Information overload is a real thing. Most of us don't have the time read research from the oceans of data available online. Subscribing to publications and specific authors from the most relevant blogs and publications is a good alternative if you have limited time to perform various online searches to find information. You can also subscribe to industry trade journals, participate in forums and discussion boards, search websites and blogs, and listen to podcasts and online videos. Leverage your personal influencers as well by networking with business leaders within or adjacent to your personal network and take the time to talk with entrepreneurs and business influencers on a frequent basis.

Questions for Reflection

- Looking at today's digital trends, what area do you want to learn more about?
- Once you've completed your research, how would you define your unique perspective on the topic?
- Who are the top influencers in your specific industry? How might you begin to network with them?

NINE

Step 4: Cultivate Your Multiple Intelligences

In this new economy, business leaders can benefit from digital workers who cultivate their own unique combination of intelligences to unleash abilities that are beyond self-imposed limitations. In this chapter, we address the collective power of your Emotional Intelligence (EQ), Creative Intelligence (CQ), and Digital Intelligence (DQ) that together can elevate your career in ways that your technical or functional skills alone can't.

What do you think when you hear the word *intelligence*? What concept immediately comes to mind? Do you imagine the numerous IQ tests taken when you were younger?

Over the past ten years, I've studied and applied Gardner's theory of multiple intelligences by combining all the intelligence capabilities I've cultivated throughout my career and using these experiences to further shape my uniqueness and differentiation. Gardner suggests that everyone may possess multiple forms of intelligence that have the potential to be nurtured and thereby strengthened—or ignored and weakened. I too, have come to the belief that every person has a broad range of abilities and intelligences they can tap into, and once unlocked, these can help them to better understand and maximize their personal strengths, capacity, and limitless intelligence capacity.

Multiple intelligences involve abilities that are highly adaptive, whether in social, interpersonal, or personal environments. Cultivating intelligences beyond my IQ enables me to overperform in a range of leadership situations. My most recent roles have required me to activate multiple intelligences when I've had to solve complex challenges through global sensitivity and empathy, technological expertise, political savviness, cultural awareness, and a multitude of other unique skills, talents, and abilities that were required for me to be influential, effectively solve problems, and confidently make tough decisions.

For example, years ago I was brought into a very difficult project on the West Coast. The project had internal structural issues, customer challenges, resource allocation issues, and project team motivation challenges. At the same time the customer was extremely frustrated with our company because of the negative implications these issues had on their business. Solving all these issues required me to have a multiple intelligences mindset—a mindset that focused on bringing the EQ, CQ, and DQ intelligence frameworks together. I immediately activated my emotional intelligence to help stabilize and alleviate the customer situation. I had to activate my social engagement abilities to build and effectively manage customer relationships, build new networks across the customer's business, and establish an incredible rapport to gain advocates within the organization. I worked to find common ground, assuring them that although we made some mistakes on the project, we were committed to partnering together in order to move the programs forward and drive the right business results that were critical to the business leaders.

Then I had to demonstrate a different level of interpersonal engagement and empathy toward the internal team to assure them that I was with them every step of the way—rolling up my sleeves to dig deep to understand the gaps, challenges, and opportunities to get things back on track, leading with empathy and credibility with accountability and authority. From that creative intelligence side, I worked collaboratively with the team to envision a new resource allocation model, a program plan, timelines, and an overall roadmap aligned to the customer's needs and priorities. To assign new project resources, we looked deep and wide across breadth of our skills portfolio and considered creative ways we could incentivize high-value resources to prioritize this program. Finally, I had to tap into my creative intelligence to really sell the value of this new program. This meant conducting lots of research to design forward-thinking approaches that would empower the leadership team to get the internal investments needed to fund the initiative.

Activating multiple intelligences has become a crucial skill for me. I don't rely on only one way of learning and one way of executing. The combined intelligences come together to drive the greatest and most unique outcomes for any given situation. I execute this framework repeatedly—it just works.

Smart Digital Things Creating the Need for Multiple Intelligences

Before AI-driven robots and Machine Learning intelligence activated across all our devices, workers were hired for their deep expertise in one or two skills that were used in linear or independent workflows. For example, a manager might dictate a message, a typist would transcribe the message, the admin would manually edit and proofread, and a clerk would make copies of the message, package them in a large brown envelope and deliver the envelopes within a cart to each executive's office. In today's digital world, this legacy workflow has been replaced by voice-enabled chatbots.

Today, workers with a narrow range of skills, no matter how highly developed, are a potential long-term liability. Organizations that have the edge and keep the edge are those that recognize the need for more intelligent workers.

Economic competitiveness depends on having the smartest workforce possible. Businesses who want to survive and grow need to be open to new ways of uncovering and developing their employees' abilities. Profiting from multiple intelligences in the workplace turns Howard Gardner's forward-thinking theory of multiple intelligences into user-friendly tools for understanding and assessing success in everyone. It provides a complete system for:

- **Emotional Intelligence**—the ability to understand and control your own feelings, and to understand the feelings of others and react to them in a suitable way
- **Creative intelligence**—the ability to deal with an unfamiliar problem or situation and coming up with a novel solution
- **Digital intelligence**—the sum of social, emotional, and cognitive abilities that enable individuals to face the challenges and adapt to the demands of life in the digital world

Increase Your Emotional Intelligence (EQ)

Emotional intelligence (EQ) is your capacity to be aware and in control of your emotions, enabling you to handle your relationships with empathy. It is the ability to express yourself appropriately with an awareness of how your emotions impact and affect others. It's the ability to discern between various feelings and choose to express them appropriately in any environment. Your emotional intelligence helps guide decision-making, aids thinking and behavior, and adapt to environments with agility. Your EQ allows you to refine or adjust your emotions in real time in order to influence the environment or to make the people around you better.

Although Michael Baldock first coined this term in a research paper in 1964, it was science journalist Daniel Goldman who brilliantly refined and operationalized emotional intelligence within a practical framework consisting of five foundational components: self-awareness, self-regulation, motivation, empathy, and social skills. Combining these components will enhance your professional and personal relationships. As artificial intelligence continues to become pervasive in every area of business and our lives, having unique, differentiated human attributes like those in EQ is even more valuable for us.

While it's important to continue to improve our human intelligence, it's equally important to balance all of this by cultivating a strong emotional intelligence. As technology continues to shift, we see the increased automation of tasks and jobs, as machines perform more and more tasks that humans once performed. However, there are still many things that machines are unable to do and that humans do better—and emotional intelligence is where we shine.

Take, for instance, the human's ability to solve highly complex problems, using many dimensions of intelligence. Machines can be configured and coded to take in lots of information and then, through algorithms, develop an outcome or recommendation. However, deep, critical analysis requires discernment—and that takes wisdom. EQ requires wisdom for complex, intuitive decision making.

We must never underestimate our power in this complex digital era. Deeply understanding situations requires EQ. We have an opportunity to listen with empathy and take in other hidden layers of information to help solve specific complex problems. Putting one's feet into another person's shoes, through empathy, is something that a machine cannot do.

The rules of human engagement continue to be transformed through an increase in remote work and virtual teams. The fact that companies are using artificial intelligence to replace many jobs makes cultivating a high EQ even more important; it's a key competitive advantage. Today's workforce is no longer about your ability to perform a task with efficiency—AI can do this much better than humans. It's about how you can leverage your high EQ to collaborate with, inspire, and influence others to lead.

It's about having a growth mindset, being adaptable to change, being resilient, and creating optimism around you. I've found that one of the best gifts I can give to everyone around me is to continue becoming more aware of how I make others feel. When I'm presenting a new idea, I want to be aware of how that impacts the people around me, careful not to step on others as I climb the ladder to elevate my career. I want to know that I'm sharing and being open and bringing others along the journey with me.

I also want to leverage the strength of those around me, empowering them to become better at what they do. For those who fear digital technology, I tap into my EQ to empower them through patience, understanding, and empathy. I address their fears, help them along, and equip them to become highly successful digital leaders. In short: As humans, emotional intelligence is our superpower.

Self-Awareness

It all starts with self-awareness—our ability to recognize and understand our own emotions and how our emotions affect others. This awareness allows us to respond consciously and responsibly to any event that comes our way. Our ability to be self-aware allows us to redirect any negative thoughts and emphasize those thoughts that breathe life into our circumstances positively.

Self-awareness is the foundation upon which all the other components of EQ rely. Once you become aware of the impact your emotions have on your behavior, you can start to manage your emotions in a way that benefits you.

Part of being self-aware is knowing the importance of maintaining a healthy work-life balance.

I realized the importance of being deeply aware of my own emotions during the 2020 pandemic, when many unsettling events occurred within a matter of a year—from social injustice issues to dealing with feelings of helplessness when I couldn't help my family. When deaths occurred on my husband's side of the family, it was hard not being able to get on a plane to visit anyone, attend a funeral to pay our respects, and to grieve with those who needed us in person.

Things like these things are tough to battle, but I still had to show up for my work colleagues. To still be a unicorn—a person who is differentiated and can handle situations with great strength and balanced emotions—I had to draw from deep within to show up at a time when I had my own personal hurts and pains to deal with. I had to find ways to translate that energy into something positive for the people around me who needed me.

It has become more and more important for me to understand my impact on the people around me. How do I show up every day for others? What is my energy level? I've always kept in mind that so many people are lost and having challenges getting through these extraordinary and uncertain times. So, when I walk into a room—or now these days participate in a virtual call—my ability to be self-aware is critical.

I perform daily introspection each evening before bedtime through meditation. It allows me an opportunity to reflect and be vulnerable—to be transparent so I can see my own personal bias in each situation and begin to develop a strategy to increase my self-mastery. My goal is to attain true self-awareness in its highest form so I am available to show up to others in authentic ways as a unique, differentiated leader who truly understands the world around me.

Self-Regulation

The next part quadrant is self-regulation, or self-management—the way we control our own impulses, how we regulate our moods, and our ability to pause and to think before responding. Think about the chaotic moments that occurred in 2020: the anger that erupted around social injustices that drastically impacted the lives of African Americans, or the assaults on our Asian communities. These life-altering incidents caused us to pause, exhale, and rethink the way we show up as unique, empathetic advocates.

Or reflect on the numerous mass shootings that increased across the United States, such as the one that occurred at the Colorado supermarket where many lives were lost in a matter of seconds. How are these events reshaping our workplace conversations? We must discover new ways to make room for tough, vulnerable conversations, and lead discussions with others through grace, peace, and authenticity.

As a Digital Unicorn, I want others to feel confident that when I show up to any situation, I bring a unique peaceful presence that is calming and strength empowering.

Social Awareness

Social awareness is the way we manage our relationships. It's about empathy—being able to step into the shoes of others and having a deep understanding about how others feel. It's the ability to connect deeply and emotionally.

People with strong social awareness can put themselves in another person's shoes so that person feels heard and under-stood. A big part of developing social awareness is having enough diverse life experiences to relate to wide-ranging situations and emotions. I strive daily to achieve this so I can positively affect those around me. It is important to have a genuine concern for others so I can create a strong, trusted bond with my teams, customers, partners, and anyone else I interact with.

It takes hard work to understand people with different experiences, cultures, and backgrounds. It takes time deeply understand what others are going through and to connect individualistically.

During one project I worked on, a software developer found out that he would have to admit his mother into a nursing home unless he and his siblings were able to come up with the means for his mother to remain home independently. This situation really touched my heart. So, as a unicorn leader, I knew I had an opportunity to respond uniquely and empathetically. I looked across our portfolio at all the projects this developer was leading and the upcoming deadlines for each initiative. Because he was leading quite a few projects with aggressive due dates, I asked him if he would be open to an internal team envisioning session. That way we could spend a few hours with the entire team to map out all the upcoming projects that were due within a five- to six-week time frame and come up with ideas on ways we could reallocate the resourcing or recalibrate the timelines. He agreed, and collectively the team reimagined the allocation of each project. We came up with a shared resourcing model that allowed some of the developers to split their time on various projects based on their skillsets. I allowed this developer to have a flex schedule that would give him the time he needed to spend with his family so they could explore new arrangements for his mother.

I believe that this is how high EQ shows up in a differentiated way. As a Digital Unicorn, it's not just about showing empathy; it's about going the extra mile to make EQ actionable and drive meaningful outcomes for others.

Six Ways to Improve Your EQ

Here are six things you can do to improve your emotional intelligence:

1. **Create a habit of becoming deeply aware of how you feel and understanding how you react when you're in an unfamiliar, uncertain, or stressful situation.** How do you respond? With fear? Courage? Boldness? Bravery? With a sense of defeat? The more you pay attention to your emotions and the more you understand how to control them and maintain a positive mindset, the more you can become intelligent at managing your reactions.

2. **Respond instead of react.** During instances of conflict, emotional outbursts and feelings of anger are common. The emotionally intelligent person knows how to stay calm during stressful situations. They don't make impulsive decisions that can lead to even bigger problems. They understand that in times of conflict, the goal is a resolution, and they make a conscious choice to focus on ensuring that their actions and words are in alignment with that.

3. **Utilize active listening skills.** In conversations, emotionally intelligent people listen for clarity instead of just waiting for their turn to speak. They make sure they understand what is being said before responding. They also pay attention to the nonverbal details of a conversation. This prevents misunderstandings, allows the listener to respond properly and shows respect for the person they are speaking to.

4. **Remove negativity.** Removing negativity has been a critical principle throughout my career because there are so many

forces that show up daily to tell me I can't achieve something that I'm aiming to do. If I'm facing a new, complex problem, especially in this digital era where we're facing so many unknowns, it's easy for fear to tell me I can't do this or that. We must get rid of what holds us back. We need to remove those things that keep us from thinking positively. For me, it's been critical, on a daily basis, to eliminate negative emotions that take me places I have no desire to go to. Research shows that we all have the ability to influence our minds and change our emotions and attitudes. However, we must be willing to do the hard work and deep analysis by writing down the things that are causing our negative mindset and reframe these into something positive. Positivity is the seed we must continue to plant in our minds. Amplifying the things that excite you will help you to achieve even more. We can enhance our EQ just by being mindful in the present moment. We can change our mindset every time negativity presents itself.

5. **Enhance your growth mindset.** Take the time to go deep into what you're great at (your abilities and your talents), while understanding there's still room to grow and learn. Carol Dweck, an American psychologist known for her mindset work at Columbia University Harvard University, developed the concept of a growth mindset. Carol and her colleagues became interested in how students' attitudes contributed to their ability to rebound from failure. They studied the behavior of thousands of children to understand their motivations and their resilience. They coined the terms "fixed mindset" and "growth mindset" to describe the beliefs that people have about learning and intelligence.

The team concluded that a fixed mindset was all about looking smart, but avoiding challenges, being defensive, being closed-minded, and ignoring critical feedback. A growth mindset led to a greater desire to learn by embracing challenges, being resilient, and being persistent in the face of setbacks and learning from criticism, instead of ignoring constructive criticism. Such people also glean lessons and inspiration from other people's experiences.

6. **Be approachable and sociable.** Emotionally intelligent people are approachable. They smile and give off a positive presence. They utilize appropriate social skills based on their relationship with whomever they are around. They have great interpersonal skills and know how to communicate clearly, whether the communication is verbal or nonverbal.

Many of these skills may seem to be best suited for those who understand basic human psychology. While high EQ skills may come more easily to naturally empathetic people, anyone can develop them. Less empathetic people just have to practice being more self-aware and conscious of how they interact with others.

By utilizing these steps, you'll be well on your way to an increase in your emotional intelligence level.

Unlock Your Creative Intelligence (CQ)

As emerging technologies like AI and ML continue to become more pervasive in our lives, our ability to cultivate our human ingenuity—our creative muscle—is one of the most important soft skills we can improve upon. According to the 2020

World Economic Forum Jobs report, creativity and innovation is a critical skill alongside critical thinking and problem-solving, especially as technologies like AI continue to automate repeatable routine tasks. We are at the beginning of exploring what's possible with creative digital ecosystems where we are seeing vast volumes of data converge with digital media and creative content, enabling us to share ideas that can be quickly globalized—and scaled.

Creativity plays a critical role in innovation. When creative processes combine with human ingenuity, together they can solve difficult problems and develop innovative opportunities that meet the changing market demands and the unique needs of consumers.

I see creativity as your ability to imagine new opportunities, adapt to dynamically changing situations, and use your imagination to solve complex problems. Your ability to develop and deploy your creativity will unlock incredible growth opportunities in the new economy. It's important to understand how technologies like AI and ML will change the workforce environment so you can focus on creating new opportunities in the market that AI cannot solve. In fact, AI is highly dependent on your ability to design ways the technology can be applied in the form of use cases.

As an example, consider the impact of the COVID-19 pandemic and the unexpected pivots businesses had to make in order to survive. We witnessed restaurants rapidly change their brick-and-mortar businesses to digital business models due to the social distancing mandates. We drastically changed our movie viewing habits as social distancing shut down theaters all over the world and movie studios were forced to migrate to digital content streaming. Even museums unleashed their creativity by enabling people to stream digital content so they could enjoy programs directly from home.

This is why it's so important for you to cultivate your creativity. Leaders must create new business models in order to gain the competitive advantage in this crowded market. Businesses are reinventing their sales models to adapt to changing customer behaviors that no longer rely on in-person interactions, and virtual technology has allowed these businesses to close sales through videoconferencing. What do these changes mean for you and me? Our imagination and creative abilities are needed now more than ever. Embracing your "childlike" curiosity and helping businesses and startups question the world around them until they uncover new opportunities, new ways to solve problems, and new ways to differentiate themselves in the market—this is the amazing opportunity before you. Below are four steps to cultivate your creative intelligence:

1. **Exercise your creative mind.** When you want to build muscle, you exercise or lift weights. When you want to increase your flexibility, you stretch right. We all have the ability to increase our creative output, and like any other muscle, our minds require exercise. This means you need a creative muscle workout plan—time that is pre-set on your calendar. Position yourself in a quiet, meditative space where you can generate ideas nonstop. Don't put any constraints on what comes out of your mind. Simply set aside a few hours each week to explore your creativity without boundaries. The key to make this successful is to dedicate more time in your day to engage in deep thinking,

which means unplugging from email, social media, and other activities that block your ability to think. It also doesn't hurt to schedule some physical exercise as well. A study published in the National Institutes of Health (NIH) showed that exercise helps to combat mental fog and fatigue while enhancing cognitive or intellectual performance.

2. **Write down your idea patterns.** When a creative thought comes to mind, have an idea journal handy to jot it down on paper—or use your smartphone. Continue to study your ideas and recognize patterns that are repeated and recognized using multiple senses. One method I use is playing chess. I must admit, I'm not a great chess player. I play the game so I can practice strategy and cultivate my pattern recognition abilities. Chess masters achieve this high status become of their consistent rigorous practice. Continuous practice is the only way to develop your creative pattern recognition skills.

3. **Take a break.** Deep think and practice mindfulness. Researchers have found that people who meditate thirty minutes a day for eight weeks have improved focus, memory, and cognitive flexibility. While I may not practice mindfulness thirty minutes a day, this practice is a frequent aspect of my week. Meditation enhances our creative minds and helps us to tap into the imaginative side of our brains. Northwestern University developed a Creative Brain Lab, a cognitive neuroscience lab dedicated to the study of creative problem solving. Northwestern researchers state that silence and solitude are crucial for nurturing creative discovery moments. Being still and gaining insights based on deep reflection is important to this process. I have

mental getaways multiple times per week, and I encourage others to do the same. Undisturbed time spent in mindfulness or meditation allow the creative juices to flow.

4. **Put your creative research skills to work.** Practice the art of discovering, collecting, and making sense of market information. The ability to quickly understand data and rapidly translate it into creative ideas is a superpower I continue to develop. Next it's important to understand how organize these creative ideas and connect the dots so you can be influential in helping businesses convert these ideas into to new products and services, customer experiences, and business models.

Sharpen Your Digital Intelligence (DQ)

Increasing your digital intelligence does not mean that you need to become an expert in technology, know how to code, or even have a deep understanding of technologies like AI, ML, Big Data, and IoT. You can go to YouTube to get a basic understanding of these technologies and what they mean. You can search for free online courses that will teach you the fundamentals. You can even learn how to code or program. But that's not what digital intelligence is about.

Digital intelligence is about two things: 1) your mindset and 2) your framework to continuously learn and adapt. The DQ Institute defines digital intelligence this way:

Digital Intelligence (DQ) is a comprehensive set of technical, cognitive, meta-cognitive, and socio-emotional competencies that are grounded in universal moral values and that enable individuals to face the challenges and harness the opportunities of digital life.

DQ is about your mindset, knowledge, skills, and values you've established in the digital world. Digital-ready citizens—whether business leaders, employees, or entrepreneurs—can navigate the rapidly changing digital landscape, easily adapt, and connect the dots using the oceans of data available everywhere.

By harnessing new ideas globally, representing all regions and socioeconomic backgrounds, shared innovation can drive inclusive growth and advancement in the digital economy so that no one gets left behind. However, this requires each of us to tap into our full digital potential, unlock our creative capacity, and cultivate new sets of skills and talents relevant to what digital business leaders require now.

All these new capabilities require you to take a journey to become digitally intelligent and to raise your digital quotient (DQ) so you can become more valuable to society. As a start, you must first give yourself permission to become digitally intelligent. You need to understand how to scan the market, uncover hidden insights, and translate these into unique knowledge and wisdom you can articulate and share with others so they, too, are empowered and inspired to tap into their digital capacity.

You must be able to use the research skills we discussed in the previous chapter to identify current, emerging, and future trends. Build a plan to expand your digital capacity. Then take the time to understand how to use the digital tools these businesses are investing in and be able to maximize the full use of these tools to unlock greater productivity, increase innovation, and gain a competitive edge.

Start to think about your place, your role, and your purpose in the digital world. Anyone can become digital. We all have the capacity to learn about digital things.

As workplaces are becoming more diverse, creative, open, and agile, you have an opportunity to increase your knowledge, experience, and abilities to maximize the investments being made by these companies. When we see how data, AI, and ML have opened up new worlds and possibilities, it's incredible to witness the way workplace dynamics are changing. We are moving from heavily micromanaged environments with very few opportunities to groupthink and innovate to open creative workplaces that require digital workers to innovate in ways like never before.

Businesses around the world are looking at digital transformation and what it's going to take to run a business in this new reality. They all understand that culture is what will give them a true competitive advantage.

Many of my clients are struggling with similar challenges. They are investing in new technology and digital capabilities. However, they have a shortage of people who understand how to use these digital investments in creative ways to increase competitive advantage and deliver new and differentiated customer experiences. Personally, I see the gap widening between legacy organizations that rely on traditional skills and those actively seeking the future digital skills required to maximize their digital transformation investments. Leaders are looking for motivated self-learners who can use the insights generated by volumes of data to both improve and invent new experiences, products, and services for their companies.

Now is the time to become a digital knowledge worker who has a unique lens on the market, understands the art of innovation, sheds old ways of thinking, and embraces the uncertainty of digital world. To get started, there are three areas to consider as you build your personal transformation plan to become more digital:

1. Cultivate your skills to use digital technologies in ethical, safe, and responsible ways.
2. Increase your creative abilities so you can contribute to the digital ecosystem, translating ideas into reality.
3. Work collaboratively across various networks to help solve global challenges and create new opportunities in the digital economy by increasing job growth, encouraging entrepreneurial opportunities, and creating positive, lasting impact.

Develop Your Digital Skills and Use Them Responsibly

Using digital technologies in our daily lives is the way we access information and rapidly expand our own personal knowledge. Consider the fact that we must process complex information from many sources, including online blogs, articles, social media sites, emails, and other digital mediums. To be effective with this information, we must also think in real time and translate this knowledge into meaningful outcomes. In the midst of a quickly changing digital world, I am constantly thinking of ways to keep my skills updated to stay relevant and prevent getting left behind.

Consider the plethora of new opportunities digital technologies are making possible in so many areas. Now think about the skills you should develop to be purposeful and intentional when making use of these technologies. Acquiring basic digital literacy and emotional and social skills are key to becoming a Digital Unicorn. As businesses and startups bring new digital capabilities to the marketplace, it's important to be a productive consumer and participant within the digital ecosystem.

For example, in 2021 Domino's Pizza partnered with Nuro, a startup self-driving delivering company, to deliver pizza to customers via autonomous vehicles—on-road vehicles that can sense the environment and operate without human involvement. In order for this business model to be profitable for Domino's, customers like us must have the digital skills and inspiration to place an order via mobile app, make a payment online, and interact with a robot upon delivery of the pizza. As you continue to increase your digital skills, you should also expand your ability to think critically by asking lots of relevant questions.

Autonomous vehicles need to collect and process massive volumes of data to ensure proper and safe functioning based on privacy regulations. Deep consideration for personal privacy requires deeper thinking, such as the kinds of data to be collected inside and outside of the vehicle. What data can be shared?

As a Digital Unicorn, you should be creating opportunities where one doesn't exist. Imagine creating a company that focuses on creating product specifications with prebuilt ethics assessments that can be customized based on the industry, products being sold, and use cases being implemented. Our ability to embrace out-of-the-box think-ing as we increase our digital knowledge and skills will be required for us to collectively maximize the world's digital capacity. Wust all work toward unleashing our digital capac-ity so we can continue to pour new ideas into the digital ecosystem and so consumers can continue to scale these new innovations and inventions.

Cornell University defines *digital literacy* as "the ability to evaluate, utilize, share, and create content using tech-nologies and the internet." By this definition, digital skills are any skills related to being digitally literate and having digital capacity to learn. I have taken full advantage of Massive Online Open Courses (MOOCs) such as Udemy and Open Educational Resources (OER), a public online digital library. As you become more digitally intelligent, you develop the ability to increase productivity for businesses that are making significant investments in their digital transformation initiatives. As businesses and entrepreneurs continue making large-scale investments to become more digitally capable, you and I have the ability to infuse greater creativity, foster innovation, and encourage collaboration in ways that no machine can.

Imagine becoming digitally intelligent to the point that you are no longer limited to using word processing soft-ware to electronically type up information, no longer limited to email or relying on PowerPoint to create presentations. As an up-and-coming Digital Unicorn, this is the power of going beyond basic digital skills to more advanced skills that leverage your creative capacity. As we move toward Software-as-a-Service (SaaS) business applications and Low Code—No

Code platforms that do not require coding skills, your digital mindset, creative thinking, and keen ability to connect the dots is the most effective way to build a successful career in the digital age. There are three major areas I want you to study more deeply:

- Artificial intelligence and machine learning
- Big data and analytics
- Internet of Things

First, let's take a look at very simple definitions, and then apply the acceleration of these technologies to events specifically related to COVID-19.

- **Artificial intelligence (AI)** increases the ability of machines to learn and act intelligently. **Machine learning (ML)** is a subset of AI focused on teaching computers how to learn without the need for humans to program or code specific tasks.
- **Big data analytics** is the strategy of analyzing large volumes of data collected from many sources, including social networks, videos, digital images, sensors, and healthcare records.
- **Internet of Things (IoT)** refers to the growing number of smart devices and objects that are connected to the internet. They gather and transmit data, communicate bidirectionally, and continue to fuel the growth of big data and AI.

Understanding Digital Acceleration through the 2020 Megatrend

While the 2020 pandemic negatively disrupted businesses across the globe, it also became a positive disruptive force for AI and ML. With digital intelligence, innovation, and human ingenuity coming together with oceans of data, researchers were able to rapidly identify patterns and gain insights that led to speedier research, root cause findings, and COVID-19 vaccine treatments that hit the market in months versus years. Consider the important work that the French startup Clevy.io delivered to market by launching an intelligent mobile chatbot to make it easier for people to locate official government communications and information about COVID-19. With more than three million messages delivered from mobile users, this virtual assistant answered thousands of questions and eased the resource burden of healthcare and government institutions. AI and ML continued to accelerate the digital landscape with innovations ranging from identifying COVID-19 symptoms through smart devices to gathering volumes of data on the virus strain to help build a variety of test kits. AI and ML reached its greatest breakthrough during the pandemic when drug developers and researchers used these technologies to accelerate the traditionally time-consuming cycles of clinical trials, develop the right vaccination formulas to help the body build immunity against the virus, and quickly deliver this vaccine to market.

The rapid spread of the global pandemic brought big data analytics tools and techniques to the forefront by generating massive volumes of data from the varied sources used to study, monitor, detect, and diagnose COVID-19 cases, track symptoms, perform contact tracing, aid in healthcare decisions, and accelerate clinical trials. Big data analysis involves a set of complex processes that enables one to bring data together from many sources to understand trends, patterns, correlations, and hidden connections within a particular set of data.

Finally, the Internet of Things (IoT) also became a critical technology during the pandemic. Kinsa, a San Francisco-based health technology company, used their internet-connected smart thermometer with a mobile app to collect real-time temperature data, thus enabling Kinsa to track the source of where the US pandemic cases started. This enabled healthcare organizations to mobilize the right resources to the right locations in a timely manner.

As you develop your personal digital learning framework, remember that it's not about becoming an expert for a given technology. Your goal is to develop highly effective research skills so you can understand how people are using digital technologies to solve business problems.

Create Your Online Learning Path

Although there are thousands of free online classes on the internet, we are only going to address five to help you get started. These will also be available in the resource section of this book.

I started my own journey to upskill my digital capabilities with edX, a massive open online course (MOOC) created by Harvard and MIT. It hosts a series of university-level courses across every industry discipline. More than 150 schools are participating in it. Amazon Web Services (AWS) offers free cloud training. AWS provides a full training library across disciplines and industries for learning about the cloud through free digital training, in-person classroom training, virtual classroom training, and private on-site and virtual training.

Google OnAir provides hundreds of free trainings, tools, and resources to help students and adults grow their skills, career, or business with free virtual workshops, events, and one-on-one coaching sessions, enabling you to upskill using an entire suite of digital tools. Intel AI Academy provides AI theory and hands-on activities through free courses from the Intel® AI Academy for software developers, data scientists, and students.

Microsoft also has courses on edX, and they offer a certification that costs less than two hundred dollars as of 2021. This is a great way to immerse yourself in any area you have identified as part of your purpose. You have the option to take on an observation role for the course, for which there is no cost. Or you can take the certification path. Initially, I suggest that you select the audit (participant observer) option so you can determine which courses you want to prioritize for the certification. Another key resource you'll want to take advantage of is Microsoft's AI Business School, which also has free courses. You can select your own path—from getting started with AI and creating machine learning models to using no code, creating intelligent chat bots, and more.

To learn more about the future in digital, check out Accenture's FutureLearn platform. This is a fantastic way to browse hundreds of courses to understand the fundamentals of the foundational digital skills you need. Courses range from artificial intelligence (AI) to digital marketing and NS mobile app development. FutureLearn courses also teach digital skills based on industries, such as retail and manufacturing. There are quizzes to test your knowledge so you have an idea of how you're progressing. Accenture also offers courses on non-digital topics such as politics and society, psychology and mental health, business management, and healthcare.

Udemy has more than 400 million course enrollments, with more than 130,000 courses available to students. Go to Udemy's free courses and immerse yourself in their online learning. There are coding courses as well as non-coding or low-code courses. Their offerings cover all disciplines and industries including business, finance, and accounting. Additional online websites that offer digital learning paths are Skillshare, LinkedIn Learning, Masterclass, and Udacity. You can also find hundreds of digital learning courses on Coursera's MOOC site, which was created by some computer science professors at Stanford University. Coursera offers free online courses, workshops, and on-demand streaming lecture videos from top instructors in subjects like business, computer science, data science, language learning, and more.

With all these learning opportunities, there's simply no excuse to fear technology. The world is opening up online course learning at low or no cost, with very rich content that can help you overcome the fear of not knowing and not understanding.

There are many opportunities for you to be able to place yourself on a fast learning path. The majority of these videos are also available via YouTube. If you simply go to YouTube and type in "getting started with artificial intelligence," you will easily come up with a list of courses that can walk you through the basics of any digital capability you want to learn more about.

All of this is changing the way we use our current social media tools. Typically, we would go to YouTube to for social reasons. Now, it's a matter of changing your habits and going to social media to immerse yourself in learning. There are hundreds of sites that offer free online learning. Just enter the keyword phrase "free online courses" into your selected search engine and get to work learning and doing.

Build Your Own Hands-On Lab

I am a non-developer whose success in technology for more than twenty years has been the result of my ability to innovate, build strategies for technology, analyze environments to prepare companies to become digital and architect their blueprint to bring in new technologies.

All of this—and I don't code. I configure things. I help companies dream big, uncover hidden opportunities within their business, discover new innovations, and drive incredible business results. Yes, I have taken coding classes to enhance my skill sets. However, I am not a developer, and I do not code for a living. Being digital does not require you to code. Let's expand our concept of what a digital worker looks like.

Take, for example, a home repairman who is required to continue serving his clients during a time of social distancing. A plumber can retrieve instructions on how to fix a plumbing issue by using an augmented reality (AR) app on his mobile phone that overlays step-by-step guidance (known as schematics). This plumber is also a digital worker.

Or consider a hotel employee who is assisting a customer with a virtual key system that connects to the hotel's Bluetooth system. The hotel employee is also a digital worker.

If a home healthcare consultant uses augmented reality on a mobile phone to enhance the homecare environment with data and information visualizations within interactive patient records, allowing the healthcare consultant to deliver personalized care, using real-time information from multiple healthcare systems, you guessed it: That home healthcare consultant is a digital home health worker.

As you build your plan to reinvent yourself, focus first on your purpose and your gifting, then align those to the needs of business leaders, customers, and the direction of the market.

Approaches I've Taken to Cultivate My Own Digital Skills

Nine years ago, I started with the basics: understanding the cloud. You can set up a free cloud account. For example, Google Cloud offers a free cloud subscription to get hands-on experience with its compute engine, storage, and other products (as of 2021), so you can try it out at no cost. This will allow you to learn the cloud fundamentals. If you visit YouTube and search "Google cloud free trial," you'll find video instructions on how to sign up for your free account, accompanied by free resources, as well as instructions on how set up stuff in your cloud. AWS also offers a free cloud account for up to twelve months for some of their cloud services (as of 2021).

The key to all of this is simply to learn something new to become more digitally savvy. You can activate either of the clouds and start setting up different resources. It's important to understand what's possible with cloud services, including storage and networking over the internet and many other products and capabilities available within the cloud. Awareness of cloud solutions and options gives you a clear understanding of what business cases and projects you can accomplish with cloud capabilities. This should be your first lab if you're new to the digital world.

I remember setting up my first cloud environment and being a bit afraid that I would break something. It's actually fine if you break a few things within your cloud environment because you can simply clear all the cloud resources you set up, start all over, and keep practicing. This will help you overcome the things you fear. So, this is a hands-on way for you to be able to navigate and understand the cloud. Who cares? It's your cloud environment.

One of my favorite sites that I use to coach others to understand through hands-on activities is customvision.AI, which is a part of cognitive services (a component of artificial intelligence) that enables other systems and apps to learn, speak, see, and understand. Custom vision is used in areas such as with vehicles. It recognizes objects and people when a driver stops at a stoplight. This online AI learning tool is free, and it allows you to upload images, run a machine learning model, and view the results.

To take a test drive and build no-code applications, Appy Pie provides an easy app builder for mobile apps, for both Android and iOS. I help small businesses to build apps through Appy

Pie's user-friendly drag-and-drop experience. You can initially try the service at no cost until you are ready to put the application into production for the public to use. Appy Pie allows start-up businesses build their own applications through an easy setup experience.

These new low-code and no-code solutions have reduced the barrier to entry when it comes to designing and building apps for businesses. Imagine your ability to become an expert at building applications by taking advantage of courses on the platforms I mentioned, learning more about the disciplines in your chosen industry, and up-leveling your skills—and then being able to help organizations build applications without ever learning how to code. That's exciting! This is what being a Citizen Developer or Citizen Innovator and a Citizen Creator is all about. You can do your research each year to look at the top no-code platforms for that specific year and find the top ten no-code platforms that companies are adopting.

I will give you one final learning tip that you can add to your Digital Unicorn learning roadmap. It's a really cool project for you to take on: learning more about the Internet of Things (IoT). Once you complete your research and understand IoT and get a deep overview of its capabilities, you'll want to navigate to YouTube to search for the many free IoT beginner courses. After you complete one of these basic courses, you'll want to try out what you've learned in a hands-on lab environment. You can start with something simple, like monitoring temperature data in the cloud from a Raspberry Pi device—a credit card-sized single board computer that can do everything a PC can do. I started my initial IoT training with a very simple project to connect a Raspberry Pi to Azure cloud and Azure

IoT hub, where I could send temperature data from a sensor to the cloud. By watching a YouTube video on connecting a Raspberry Pi to Azure IoT, I was able to get through the step-by-step training to connect a device to the cloud.

Why is this an important lesson to learn? Well, imagine that you're able to control your TV by using your iPhone as a remote control. Or envision your ability to turn the lights and air conditioning on and off remotely, from *anywhere,* through a mobile app on your phone.

The key is not whether you succeed or fail in your lab experiment. It's about getting hands-on experience and removing the fear of trying something new that you've never done before. When you're completely immersed in your learning, you can better connect to what's possible, and you'll no longer fear what you don't understand.

Overcoming the Fear of Trying New Things

I'm always reminded of a famous quote from Tuvok, *Star Trek* Voyager's second officer and chief of security who said, "We often fear what we do not understand; our best defense is knowledge." This key wisdom principle has guided my entire career. The only way I can overcome the fear that comes with uncertainty, especially in the innovation world that I have been a part of for more than twenty years, is to learn—and not just by reading.

You cannot imagine the number of innovations I've created that have failed. Too many to name in this book, and I've learned from all of them. Failure is my classroom as well as a very effective teacher, allowing me to overcome and successfully triumph over the ambiguous, the unknown, and the uncertain. Failure has been integrated into my successes.

I love the quote from Marianne Williamson' poem, "Our Deepest Fear," that says "Our deepest fear is not that we are inadequate. Our deepest fear is that we are powerful beyond measure." This is so true. We fear many times what's possible within us because we don't understand how powerful we are in our own right. Once the light bulb turns on, we get a deeper understanding of something we had absolutely no understanding of prior, and our power becomes limitless in that specific area. And, yes, truthfully that can be a bit scary, especially when you don't understand how great your power is. You have to go beyond learning and really be attuned to immersive learning. The term *immersive* is related to any activity that occupies most of one's attention, time, or energy. Another definition says that *immersive* means "to engage deeply and wholly."

It's also important to understand the purpose of these digital capabilities. You don't have to become an expert, and I think many times that's the pressure that so many of us put on ourselves. I've learned that it's important just to understand the capability and the power of digital and then use your personal framework to connect the dots with your purpose and how you should be making your mark in this space with your unique gifts and talents.

So, instead of avoiding certain jobs because you lack the technology skills you feel are needed to be successful, you can obtain such jobs by immersing yourself in training and online courses, online learning videos, and other free training resources available on the internet. This is the open doorway for us to enter into new roles and occupations and start new businesses— becoming entrepreneurs in areas we could never even have imagined a decade ago.

Korn Ferry research shows that by 2030 we will have a worldwide talent shortage that could reach more than 85 million people, with an economic impact costing trillions of dollars globally. And although the demand for technical skills like coding and mobile app development will continue to increase, there are other skills that involve low coding and automation that will also continue to skyrocket.

Questions for Reflection

- What are some practical ways you can be more approachable and sociable, thus increasing your emotional intelligence?
- How can you create space in your life to set aside time each day to practice meditation and mindfulness with the goal of increasing your creative intelligence?
- When can you start to build your digital intelligence by gaining a deeper understanding of current, emerging, and future tools and trends and how businesses are using these tools, and how will you make time for this exercise with such a busy schedule?

TEN

Step 5: Deploy Yourself

Now that you have the right digital mindset, you have a set of behaviors and habits that can move you toward your destination: your new digital career. You've performed your research, applied your new knowledge, and conducted your own hands-on lab. It's now time to deploy your gifts and everything that you've learned by putting it into practice in a real-world environment. It's time to empower others to solve complex problems and get feedback on your progress.

Although it's important to be employed—meaning that you seek work and get paid by an employer for the work you do—it's even more important to become deployed—meaning that your gifts are so attractive to the world that businesses, communities, or governments utilize them to empower their vision and mission.

While you can be laid off or let go from a job when you're employed, when you're deployed, although you momentarily may not have a salaried role, no one can ever lay you off from your gifts, talents, skills, or purpose. When you're deployed, you can still tap into many areas of your network, no matter what happens from a macro level in the economy. You can simply *re*deploy your gifts, talents, skills, or purpose to the next place where you can add value.

That's why it's so important to stay ahead of the trends happening in the digital world and keep your skills not only up-to-date, but next level. It is also important to build a powerful and actionable network around yourself.

Whether you are working for a startup company, a corporation, or a nonprofit or you're an entrepreneur, the digital era provides many opportunities for you to deploy your in-demand skill set and your perspective.

When I've learned something new and need to put it into practice, I've identified seven areas where I can deploy myself in order to use and further sharpen that skill:

- Volunteering
- Presenting at a social or community event
- Writing and posting a blog piece
- Taking on a stretch project that taps into skills you haven't mastered yet and challenges you, creating an opportunity for growth
- Creating a video blog and posting it to a website or social media platform
- Presenting at industry conferences

The first great place to start is skills-based **volunteering**. The Volunteer Match website is an easy way to align your skills to the needs of nonprofits all over the world. This rapidly growing corporate citizenship program focuses on bringing together talent from corporations, startups, and nonprofits, as well as individual entrepreneurs, to help solve complex problems.

Examples range from building applications to filling the holes in a digital skill set that a nonprofit organization lacks among its own employees. It's a great way for you to work on real-world projects and expand your skills while volunteering your time to help others.

You will become a project consultant to these nonprofits and have the ability to select from many projects, taking the skills you've learned and applying them to critical business needs for these nonprofits. These opportunities provide you with an environment to practice your craft.

This will also give you a chance to put your newly learned skills to work, and gain the experience needed to continue progressing your career. I've participated with Volunteer Match and assisted many nonprofits in the areas of AI and IoT.

For one project, I helped to create a platform that used sensor technology to facilitate independent living opportunities for the elderly. I've also helped start-up businesses that are receiving business development assistance from nonprofits to build no-code applications and websites for their businesses.

This allowed me to connect the dots and understand the practical application of my skills and how businesses use them. It enabled me to develop a broader strategy for how I could help other businesses embrace these new digital capabilities and how to apply them across their businesses to expand their footprint and presence in their sector.

A second thing that I do once I've learned something new is to **present at a social or community event**. I'm a part of many social communities within LinkedIn, and I've volunteered my time and created a webinar to share my new knowledge with those in a particular community to help their professional development. When I do such events, I keep the feedback circle small, limiting it a small number of registrants. I welcome participants' feedback. This is a great way to test, practice, and deploy your knowledge to new groups or to groups you're currently interacting with as a thought leader.

The third way that I put my knowledge into practice is by **writing blog posts**. LinkedIn, where you can easily write about a topic and get immediate feedback, is great for this. You can hear from a wide variety of professionals and interact with them in the comments section. This puts you on people's radar, helps establish your credibility as a budding expert in that area, and strengthens and broadens your personal and professional network. If you do an excellent job, those who attended may bring up your name as someone knowledgeable on the topic you've presented on when they're speaking to people in their own networks.

The fourth way I demonstrate new knowledge is by **taking on strategic stretch projects** or hands-on technology projects for startup companies that need the support. I'm able to engage in real-world projects, offering my services on a volunteer basis so I can get the skills and experience in a more immersive way. Taking on a stretch project within your current company is another great way to get skills; you can volunteer to work on a project within another department, thus going beyond your current job responsibilities.

Another way to put your knowledge into practice is by **presenting at industry conferences**. I google the phrase "conference speaker submissions" along with the year I want to speak and the topic that I would like to talk about—for instance, digital transformation. This allows me to discover all the upcoming digital transformation conferences and then can write a summary and submit a topic to present at an industry event. This is a great way to be recognized, and it gives you the opportunity to be on a platform that really forces you to continue studying.

Finally, something that I always recommend is that once you have all the digital assets you've produced from these activities—presentations, blog posts, videos, etc.—it's important to put them on a website as part of your portfolio. By putting links to all of your assets, you have something of value you can present to potential employers or clients, use to demonstrate your expertise for speaking gigs, and make accessible to other people interested in you and your work. These are all ideas to deploy yourself beyond your day-to-day employment. The key is to stay relevant, be marketable, and rise above the changes that are occurring around you.

Expand Your Influence

The word *influence* means to become a compelling force that impacts others' behavior, actions, or opinions. Expanding your influence means to increase your ability or capacity to have an effect on others. Imagine that you now have this new set of skills and abilities that you're able to use to influence and attract new mentorship, business coaches, or sponsors. These are individuals who can potentially bring you into an organization and open up new windows of opportunity for you. They can help you to become influential across social communities, industries, nonprofits, startups, and new professional networks that will power the next level of your personal transformation in this digital economy. Imagine being part of a startup that wants to pay you to be a consultant for them, based on the skills you have to offer.

My goal is to continue to become an impactful influencer in business and technology. Influencers have followers and a voice in the industry—they also lead and set direction for others. Establishing yourself as an influencer is incredibly important to build a powerful reputation and credibility, which directly translates to unstoppable success.

The key is to continue your lifelong knowledge path. After

all, how can you influence others without being an expert or go-to person in your industry? Real influencers never stop learning within their professional or personal lives.

Then, leverage your new knowledge and unique perspectives to be more influential and attract an entirely new professional network of business advocates, including coaches and mentors who can help accelerate the next level in your professional career.

Build an Actionable Network

It has been important for me to have supportive alliances personally and professionally in order to accelerate the achievement of my life goals and professional goals. Having the right advice from a purpose-driven network of mentors—my personal board of directors—is truly an indispensable resource.

My network is ever evolving as I continue gaining the skills to progress in my digital career. One of the core reasons that I am able to build such a sophisticated network is that I don't go in thinking only about what's in it for me. I think about all the areas I want to impact. I do a lot of research, and now LinkedIn has made it much easier to create the right network that fits this season of my career.

That said, I don't go in empty-handed. My goal is always to ask how I can empower everyone in my entire network. How can I empower each and every individual with the skills I've learned? How can I serve and be of value?

Hence, the concept of building a powerful personal board

of directors has been a critical part of my career growth, especially as a woman in technology. My personal board acts as my sounding board. They provide me with feedback on career decisions I'm making. They are there to consult with and advise me, and to help me understand the opportunities and challenges, especially on this path of leadership.

That's why it's important that I talk with C-Suite executives, business leaders, and entrepreneurs. This collective intelligence I'm gathering helps me to stay on the best track to remain up-to-date with my skills and ride any headwinds of change—rather than be battered by them. It also helps me expand my circle of influence.

Don't limit your personal board of directors. It can be composed of friends who have accelerated their career paths. I consult my best friend, and we take classes together on topics that help us to accelerate our digital capacity so we can keep each other encouraged and motivated. I have mentors who have turned into sponsors as they have risen up the chain of command and now sit in executive seats. They still advise me and help me to understand their journey so I can continue to progress in my own journey.

I have business coaches, mentors, and career advisors who are very seasoned colleagues. They continue to guide me as they accelerate in their own careers. It's important to develop a diverse network of people so you have a pool of talented thinkers with different experiences, backgrounds, and digital or business capabilities.

How do I build these networks in the first place? I start with what we talked about early in the book: a deep understanding of my purpose and the value I bring to the table. I also need to understand the different areas of my network that I want to grow and where each person fits into the structural makeup of my personal board of directors. You want to attract the right people to play the right role within your career.

How often do I meet with each member of my personal board? It might be once a month. So, communicating my expectation to them and getting agreement on the role they will play is extremely helpful in tracking progress. Long-term advisors can play different networking roles over the course of my career. I know that my long-term mentor will support my development by providing real-time feedback, advice, and guidance. Typically, this is someone who inspires me.

Seeking potential mentors is not as difficult as it might seem. Over the course of my career, I've found mentors within companies I've worked for. I've also found mentors within community groups, especially in my LinkedIn community. Likewise, through nonprofit organizations where I've volunteered, I've gained incredible mentors and coaches who have helped with my growth and development. You can also seek mentoring services from universities, Chambers of Commerce, or even within your social or religious groups.

To build and attract the right mentor network, you must be purposeful, deliberate, and intentional. As a first step, I write down specifically what I'm seeking in a mentor, the outcomes I desire, and how the mentor can add value to my career—or life. This is an important step since every mentor or coach will serve a different purpose.

I work to understand the specific goal that I want to

accomplish. For instance: I would like to become a better communicator. So, as I approach a potential mentor for specific help on that, I'll say something like: "I really enjoy the way that you communicate when you're presenting. I would love to connect with you for a few brief sessions to learn more about your leadership journey since I am taking a similar path. May I schedule an initial thirty-minute meeting, and then we can discuss your availability to have a few more rapid coaching sessions during the year?"

Although I'm very specific about the support I need, I also want to be thoughtful and not overwhelm individuals since it's likely they are asked frequently to mentor others. I want my approach to stand out. I like being set apart and memorable. I try various approaches to attract mentors in order to be unique and differentiated.

The other important thing is that I know the areas I want to improve in, and I'm intentional about approaching the right mentors where there is shared purpose and outcomes. So do your homework. Be sure to research and get to know your mentor through their social and business networks. Then spend the time connecting the dots so your opening conversation immediately resonates with them.

Another type of mentor I have on my personal board is someone who is very well connected and can open doors for me. This person is often referred to as a rainmaker—an influencer with a large social network who can bring other mentors into my world, someone who can make introductions and truly help me grow my network. To activate this type of mentor, I must have something of value to offer. I look for areas to align my gifts, skills and experience with something this mentor can utilize and appreciate. Also, such contacts usually become more willing to open doors for me and increase my connections by sharing their connections.

The next person is a business coach. I have several business coaches helping me on my leadership journey. It is important to continue to become attractive through your knowledge, wisdom, intelligence, and digital capacity. All those things, combined with a coach, can help you to develop your influencer skills.

Business coaches will give you the tough, straight-shooter advice you need. They're looking at things from a top-level vision, and they can shed light on how to navigate through some really complex situations. They help sharpen your skills and motivate you, especially through difficult choices and seasons. Finally, I have a quite a few sponsors as well. Often a sponsor may start out as your mentor, coach, or someone you're doing a stretch project for. You don't choose your sponsors— your sponsors choose you. A sponsor speaks up for you and advocates for your advancement—even, and perhaps most of all, when you're not in the room. You have to use a different approach to attract a powerful sponsor who will advocate for you. I actually take on a servant-leadership mentality, where I approach leaders, offer my skills, and express my willingness to do new projects as a stretch assignment.

I offer something I can do in my spare time that has visibility and, relative to that leader's goals, will give me great credibility when a sponsor has a role in mind that I would be great for. Staying relevant and top of mind is what you want to strive for.

Fire-Up Your Fiercest Allies

Ask yourself: "Does my network contain people who inspire me to be my best self? Does this network make me even more extraordinary? Do the people in this network challenge me to move to new levels of my digital journey?"

Take a good inventory of everyone you've listed as a potential mentor, business coach, career advocate, sponsor, or a friend who will take this journey with you and ask you tough questions you may not ask of yourself. Be prepared to remove those who don't add value to your journey and go deeper to discover those who will add the most value.

Have you selected people who are genuine and a good match for your personality? Have you only enlisted "Yes" people? Or have you included individuals who will be authentic, truthful, and give you constructive criticism, even when it's painful?

Now I'll share how I activate my allies—those people who will be my strongest and fiercest career advocates. This is about your personal advisors and your coaches coming together on your behalf to help accelerate your success, so you can thrive in this digital era.

Steps for Approaching Your Potential Board of Directors

Reach out either via email or LinkedIn and request a brief, fifteen-minute introductory meeting. I don't ask directly for that individual's mentorship. Instead, I state that I have seen the great things they are achieving, and I would like to have fifteen minutes of their time to learn more about their strategy, long and short-term goals, what's important to them, and how I can support them to accelerate achieving their goals for that year.

Open the relationship by complimenting your new connection and share what you've learned about them in your research. The initial call gives you an opportunity to ask how you can be of service, but it also lets you gauge, based on that fifteen-minute conversation, if this person is a good fit as a potential mentor.

If there's great chemistry, then ask for a follow-up forty to forty-five minute meeting, so you can learn more about how you might support them in the interim and continue to learn from that individual. Keep this informal because busy professionals already have so many demands on their time. What you're asking for is time well spent, where both parties are gaining value from the exchange. That's my strategy.

During the follow-up call, capture a couple of areas where you can be of value to that individual, and then specifically tell them that you are interested in having him or her as a mentor and explain what that means: thirty to forty-five minutes of that person's time at least once every quarter, so you can simply listen to how they do their strategic planning and how they've been successful. A commitment to connect once every three months allows for more flexibility without all the pressure to spend too much time with you. In return, you're bringing something to the table as well: you're gifting them with low-hanging fruit doesn't require a lot of effort on your part. It is an exchange.

Mentors also love to know that you are immediately applying their guidance. So, at every mentor meeting, you'll want to show progress from your last meeting and how you're paying forward what you've learned from that mentor. This really inspires your mentors to continue meeting with you, because they see a direct impact and visible fruit.

What's the secret to taking your mentor relationships to the highest degree? It's how you inspire them and pay attention to the things that they're achieving. It's also taking the time to deeply understand their goals and objectives by visiting their websites and being aware of their upcoming speaking events. And when they give you feedback and guidance, take note so you can show evidence of how you acted on the advice they took the time to share. In exchange, you should share the insights and perspectives you're seeing in business, industry, or technology—the information you are discovering from your research. This is another way to not only add value to your network, but to put your newly learned knowledge and skills into practice.

Finally, continue to be an energetic force, bringing positivity into your mentor's world. Remember, people with positive presence are easy to be around. From the famous words of Maya Angelou, "People will forget what you said. People will forget what you did. But people will never forget how you made them feel." It's your energetic spirit that fires up your mentor network, driving them to continue working on your behalf, because they see the fruit, outcomes, and results of their efforts.

You can go a step further, and—after a few sessions— put together a one- or two-slide presentation showing clear evidence and measurement of your progression since your mentorship relationship started. This gives your mentor proof that things they have done to help you are working.

Many of us don't have money to invest in a formal business coach that involves paying on an ongoing basis. It can get quite expensive. However, there are business coaches who will volunteer their time to help you. They may not be as available as a paid coach. However, to tap into whatever resources are available to you at your current level and budget, you will need to do your research. Use a search engine to locate business coaches who will work with you at a very low cost—or no cost. I recommend going after business coaches who provide a free consultuation for you to learn about their services. During the consultation, be very specific about the area of growth that's important to you and ask if they offer a sliding scale or "pro bono" coaching (that is, coaching for free). If they don't, ask if they can recommend other coaches who do volunteer coaching. Be aware that certified coaches have to keep up with their certification, including the number of times that they're delivering coaching, so they often have to get very creative to keep up with these requirements.

If you can't get a coach who fits your budget, DIY it and visit the website, blog, and free coaching materials offered by a coach you admire but can't afford—and take advantage of that coach's free materials through self-guidance. Many times this can be almost as effective as a paid coaching engagement. Also, don't shy away from business coaches who are not certified. If they have years of experience in the area of interest important to you, focus on the value these individuals can bring to your development and the significance of their network influence.

Now, the risk is that you get back what you invest. This means that if you are seeking a level of business coaching that will catapult your career to new levels, it's important to be intentional about investing in yourself as a priority. I understand that with many financial obligations, investing in yourself is not an easy decision, but it's one that will pay great dividends.

Finally, advocates and allies you want to activate are potential sponsors. Remember, you are chosen by your sponsor, but the key is to surround yourself with a very rich network of influencers and thought leaders who can guide your progress in your role at any enterprise organization, startup, or nonprofit. So, the goal for you is to continue learning, researching, walking in your purpose, and deploying your gifts—and you will attract phenomenal networks that you can add to your own personal board of directors.

Become the Go-To Guru

Becoming the go-to person for certain things at work or within my social network is another goal I strive for. People want to do business with someone who has a great reputation, is credible, and an expert in their field.

I've spent a lot of time working in innovation, including AI, big data, mixed reality, and other emerging technologies. Many times people reach out to me through LinkedIn to ask my opinion or guidance on where the future market is going in terms of innovation and emerging technologies. I realize that as I increase my knowledge and expertise in a given topic or domain, the more I'm seen as a "go-to" expert, which helps me to gain the credibility, respect, and trust needed to increase my value to others. Take a moment to consider what you are really good at. What comes naturally to you? What are your areas of expertise? Once you understand your natural abilities, it's important to grow these abilities so you attract people who need what you have to offer—something unique that only you can deliver to the market. Developing such expertise takes consistent and focused effort. The more knowledge and wisdom you acquire, the more attractive you become to the business world.

The key is to differentiate yourself so that you are a uniqu standout. You want to become known as someone who has a different perspective and the ability to see opportunities others miss. That's the reason why people will come to you: because of your *unique* way of seeing the world.

Never stop learning. Continue to learn and share your point of view across social platforms. Connect your purpose to what you're passionate about in the digital world, the topics that move and inspire you. Then continue to go deeper: Ask more questions and study to learn patterns and be able to differentiate yourself through your unique observations, analysis, and actionable solutions. Become known as a go-to person, problem solver, and visionary.

Keep a growth mindset and be open-minded about absorbing new information from many places by reading blogs from different companies and organizations, noting what's top of mind for them. Being able to keep your pulse on the market by studying an industry that interests you and doing deep-dive research creates an opportunity for you to become a dot connector and thought leader.

Another step to become the go-to person is by developing the ability to anticipate the market and make predictions about the future—by having foresight and insight based on your research, intelligence, and wisdom. Working to develop this muscle provides a great opportunity for you to begin positioning yourself as someone who can help businesses, nonprofits, and community organizations to anticipate what's to come in the digital future.

Next, you can build a summary profile, documenting the experience and acumen that has helped you to become the go-to person on certain topics. You can do this via your bio, resume, or social media pages so that you are visibly recognized as a person who is a thought leader in a specific part of the digital landscape.

Finally, mentor others. Paying it forward is critical, because this is also a great way for you to continue to build your reputation and attract opportunities to provide guidance to rising stars in your industry or other industries. You can also be the door opener and give someone an opportunity who might *never* have that opportunity otherwise based on that person's background. People who have such opportunities become the "first" in their families, or communities, to do so. But thanks to your opening that door, they hopefully won't be the last!

Some people like to share the fruits that come from paying it forward on their social media pages, and this helps them to continue to grow their brands. Others don't like being in the limelight and prefer to do their good works behind the scenes. Do what is most comfortable for you—there's no wrong or right way to do good. Investing in your learning and sharing your knowledge and cultivating wisdom with others will help you to accelerate their digital career paths—and yours.

Questions for Reflection

- Decide on three key ways you will deploy yourself and your in-demand skills. Will it be volunteering, writing a blog post, or presenting at an industry conference, or some other way that will give you visibility and expand your influence?
- What initial steps will you take to develop your personal "board of directors"?
- Who could you offer to mentor on your journey to become a go-to guru in your industry?

PART III: DELIVER IRRESISTIBLE VALUE EVERYWHERE

ELEVEN

Become a Person of Value

The term *value* means that something is important or has worth. Value also refers to something that is excellent or useful—an indicator of worth. Value defines quality and determines the level of influence and impact you can achieve.

It is my personal goal to be a person of value and to continue to increase my value every place I show up. This means that I light up every room I walk into with my purpose, passion, wisdom, and intellect. People are attracted to people who are valuable and bring something to the table. People enjoy and appreciate being around someone they learn something from and wouldn't have learned if that person hadn't shown up.

Your goal should be to add value in a way that no one else can—to introduce new levels of energy, positivity, connection, and authenticity in the spaces you occupy.

This also means translating your skills and insights into value that a business leader can apply to become more competitive, compelling, and powerful. When you interact with others, your goal is to offer new knowledge, information, and relevant data and contribute a fresh perspective.

Being valuable starts with you. It begins with your own personal development, transformation, and growth. You must continue to grow in intellect, emotional intelligence, creative intelligence, digital intelligence—and in your gifting and purpose.

If you want achieve the next level and continue to set yourself apart, self-development and growth must be a part of your daily schedule. As you continue to sharpen your skills and put them into practice and evolve as a thought leader, expert, and recognized go-to person in your field, your value will increase exponentially.

To get started, take an inventory of your strengths and weaknesses. You can use the content from this book to help identify key focus areas and leverage online assessments such as "Strength Finders" to evaluate the maturity of your skills. For your EQ, research assessments that help you measure your self-awareness, self-regulation, motivation, social awareness, and social regulation. To understand some areas to improve for digital intelligence, you can review the DQ Framework, which includes digital literacy, digital skills, and digital readiness competencies approved by the IEEE Standards Board.

Your personal transformation journey does not have to be an expensive one. There is so much information available online that you can simply choose a topic, then perform research using the steps learned in this book to find the right whitepapers, blogs, learning videos, and books. For example, what would happen if you decided to learn a new skill each year?

Let's say you want to learn how to configure low code-no code mobile applications so you can build a consulting practice to help customers design business process apps that give them market differentiation. You would start by performing market research to understand which industries are using low code-no code platforms and identify the use cases, as well as the potential addressable market.

Next, you would go deeper to study the industries and how they are implementing use cases. What outcomes are they driving with low code-no code? How are they empowering their customers to achieve more in their business? You begin to ask questions so you can develop new ideas that can solve problems that have yet to be addressed.

Then you can search for low code-no code free trials to gain hands-on experience. You can navigate to YouTube to search for the low code platform vendor and review any training or marketing videos to learn more. Finally, you deploy your talent in this area by volunteering your time at a startup company or nonprofit organization to build low code-no code applications that deliver value to these entities, while posting an inspiring blog to show off your thought leadership skills in this emerging market.

I've been practicing techniques to reinvent my skills since I was in my early twenties and have found it to be an incredible value lever throughout my career. Here are examples of some of the topics I've studied in depth and cultivated skills for:

- Business Architecture
- Business Process Management and Reengineering
- Project Management
- Digital Transformation
- Cloud Solutions Architecture
- Strategic Planning
- Mergers and Acquisitions
- Finance Strategy
- Organizational Behavior and Change
- Sales Strategy
- Coaching and Mentoring Techniques
- Meeting Planning and Management
- Communication Techniques
- Presentation and Speaking Skills
- Listening Skills
- Leadership

- Emotional Intelligence
- Mindfulness Training

I've found throughout my life that the more I learn, the more I realize how much I don't know. The best way I know to improve myself and increase my value—whether as an employee or the owner of a startup—is to always keep learning and growing. I treat my career as a business and myself as a competitive product to be continuously improved, year after year.

Over many years of being at the edge of innovation, I've realized that my success is not about my own personal performance and what I think about the quality of work I'm delivering—it's about how others perceive the value I am providing.

Throughout my career, I've always made it my personal mission to deliver greater value than I receive. And this has certainly separated me from the pack, allowing me to deepen my relationships across my network, because people see my authenticity and willingness to serve first—instead of seeking first to be served.

In the book *The Art of Manliness,* Brett and Kate McKay share that "when you create instead of consume, your capacity for pleasure increases, as opposed to your need for it. Being a creator gives you far more lasting and deeply satisfying happiness than consuming ever will."

This is such a powerful and insightful statement.

When you invest in yourself, grow your intelligence and digital skills, and translate all you've learned into meaningful and actionable insights for businesses and communities, you spark an incredible level of value that attracts others to you.

Here are four areas I focus on to continue becoming a person of even greater value:

1. Commit to being valuable and deliver. Being a person who does what they say they will do is critical for people to trust you and depend on you to get stuff done. Have I taken the extra step? Have the outcomes I've delivered truly added value to the person or company receiving them?
2. Pour into the lives of others and help without always expecting something in return. It gives me joy to see others accelerate their careers. Whenever I feel any envy, I ask myself, "Why am I having these thoughts and feelings?" We must continuously keep our egos in check; sometimes human nature is such that we want to see others get ahead—but not ahead of *us*. Deeply examine and find the root of such feelings—so you can correct them and continue to be a champion and genuine supporter of others.
3. Be authentically vulnerable. This is critical, particularly when we miss the mark, make a mistake, or fail. We should be able to admit (publicly and privately): "You know what? I did not measure up. This didn't work out, but failure is my classroom. So, let's go back to the drawing board and try again." That authentic mindset and attitude helps to generate the right energy—even when things are not going well.
4. Appreciate everyone around me. I consistently let them know that they are valued and appreciated, that I pay attention to the things they do. I'm very specific in making sure they understand that I acknowledge them and the great

work that they do. All these things combined together, cultivated, put into practice, and repeated over and over help me to increase my value to others.

Increase Your Attraction

When you show up, are you a burden or a light? Are you easy to interact with?

These are the areas I really focus on and strive to radiate when I show up. I don't want to be viewed as a burden in my personal and professional life. I want to have the right mindset and be deliberate and intentional in my choices and actions.

What does creating value for others look like? Do you do what you say you're going to do? Can people believe that your word is your bond? When given a deadline, can you meet or exceed it? Do you also return deliverables not just on time, but with excellence? Do you respond to your emails in a timely manner—within twenty-four to forty-eight hours? Or do you ignore them until someone follows up—and that someone is often irritated? Being dependable and accountability matter.

Do you treat every person who emails you with the same degree of value, or do you ignore some emails completely based on where that person is sitting in an organization or at in his or her career? Do you assign more value to people who are senior level and less to those who are junior or support staff, like an assistant?

A value-creation mentality means having the mindset of getting stuff done. A value-creation mindset inspires people to know that they can rely on you to deliver requests and projects on time and get stuff done with excellence. Having a value-creation mindset is an opportunity to accelerate growth and development for an entire organization. It gives you credibility and strengthens your relationships with colleagues and clients. It enhances your personal effectiveness so you can attract more opportunities and accelerate your career path. People must also understand your capabilities and trust your ability to deliver value—this sets you up for success. As you are progressing through your digital journey and require support from one of your network, having these attributes increases higher-quality opportunities.

Questions for Reflection

- In what ways have you delivered on your commitments so that you've truly added value to those you've worked with?
- Think about some times when you missed the mark in some way. How can you reframe this so you can generate the right kind of energy moving forward?
- Who are you grateful for today? Take the time to acknowledge them and let them know how much you value what they do.

TWELVE

Empower Others to Succeed and Thrive

I live by the philosophy "Each One Teach One," which means that with all the experiences, knowledge, skills, and lessons, and abilities I've acquired in every area of my life, I must teach others so they can achieve even greater things in their life and career. I continue to cultivate myself so I can cultivate others, helping them to discover their purpose and unleash their greatness into the world. In fact, I truly believe the fastest way to achieve success is to help others succeed. Whether it's a business leader, entrepreneur, community group, or nonprofit organization, it's important to me that we all succeed and thrive together.

I've realized that in order for me to deliver meaningful value to others, I must understand fully what they want and be able to anticipate their future needs. Many times, when coaching others on this, someone will say that the person to whom they delivered value didn't appreciate what was delivered. The first question I always ask is: "Did you deliver what you wanted, or did you deliver the value they needed? Did you take the time to understand their needs and go deeper—to anticipate things that they didn't even ask for?"

Brian Tracy, sales training and personal success expert, said it best: "Successful people are always looking for opportunities to help others. Unsuccessful people are always asking, 'What's in it for me?'" My greatest successes in my career have come because I am intentional about helping others to succeed.

Four Steps to Help Others Succeed

1. **Research and deeply understanding the needs of the people for whom you are delivering value.** Be sure to take advantage of all the resources you've learned in this book, starting with approaches to research, increasing your skills, deeply understanding the areas that are important to the people you're working with, and then connecting the dots to deliver above and beyond.

2. **Exceed expectations.** Once you have an opportunity to fulfill a deliverable someone entrusted you to deliver, then go the extra mile. This is about doing more than what was asked.

3. **Leverage your expertise to become someone who can support people in areas where they have gaps or lack skills.** Create time within your schedule cultivate your expertise so you can help others cultivate theirs. People will come to look to you for guidance and see you as someone who can wisely steer them in the right direction.

4. **Make others shine.** This is huge. The work you do to help others elevate their careers serves as a major opportunity to accelerate your own career—and your personal brand. Look to empower others with a good heart, a positive spirit, and no hidden motives. You simply want to inspire them to be highly successful. The key is that when you're creating and delivering value, you must be deliberate in continuing to grow in value to others. This should be a daily habit, using the principles you've learned throughout this book. Make it an intentional habit to cultivate the success of others as you cultivate your own success.

Now It's Your Turn

I hope I have both inspired you and challenged you to join the growing number of Digital Unicorns and forge new pathways to success! Refer to this book often and keep growing. Never forget, the world needs the unique gifts that only you can share!

Questions for Reflection

- How can you exceed expectations, either in your job or with a key client?
- When you think of your ideal client, how might you increase your understanding of what they truly need?
- What are some practical ways you can cultivate success in those around you and make them shine?

REFERENCES

PART 1: BECOME YOUR OWN UNICORN—STAND
OUT IN A CROWDED ECONOMY

World Economic Forum (2020). "Accelerating Digital Inclusion in the New Norm." Accessed November 20, 2021. http:// www3.weforum.org/docs/WEF_Accelerating_ Digital_ Inclusion_in_the_New_Normal_Report_2020. pdf.

Armbrecht, A. World Economic Forum (2016). "4 reasons 4 billion people are still offline." Accessed April 4, 2020. https://www.weforum.org/agenda/2016/02/4-rea-sons-4-billion-people-are-still-offline/.

Forbes (2013). "Disrupt or Be Disrupted." Accessed June 8, 2020. https://www.forbes.com/sites/ johnkotter/2013/04/03/ how-to-lead-through-business-disruption/?sh=2c734c262644

Harari, Y.N. *Financial Times,* 2020. Yuval Noah Harari. "The world after coronavirus." Accessed May 5, 2020. https://www.ft.com/content/19d90308-6858-11ea-a3c9-1fe6fedcca75 March 20.

McKinsey & Company (2021). "The new digital edge: Rethinking strategy for the postpandemic era." Accessed May 29, 2021. https://www.mckinsey.com/ business-functions/ mckinsey-digital/our-insights/ the-new-digital-edge-re-thinking-strategy-for-the-post-pandemic-era.

Gartner (2015). "Every Employee Is a Digital Employee." Accessed July 17, 2020. https://www.gartner.com/ smarterwithgartner/ every-employee-is-a-digital-employee/.

PART II: FIVE STEPS TO DISCOVER, DEVELOP, AND DEPLOY YOURSELF

World Economic Forum (2020). *The Future Jobs Report*. Accessed November 20, 2020. https://www.reskill-ingrevolution2030.org/reskill-ingrevolution/wp-content/ uploads/2020/12/ WEF_Future_of_Jobs_2020.pdf.

McKinsey & Company (2016). "Transforming operations management for a digital world." Accessed February 4, 2020. https://www.mckinsey.com/business-functions/ strategy-and-corporate-finance/our-insights/ how-covid-19-has-pushed-companies-over-the-technology-tipping-point-and-transformed-business-forever.

Deming, W. Edwards. *The New Economics for Industry, Government, Education.* MIT Press, 1994.

Howard Gardner, *Frames of Mind: The Theory of Multiple Intelligences* (New York: Basic Books, 1983).

Harvard Business Review (2016). "4 Steps to Having More 'Aha' Moments." Accessed June 15, 2020. https://hbr. org/2016/10/4-steps-to-having-more-aha-moments.

Northwestern University (2015). "Creative Genius Driven by Distraction." Accessed October 13, 2020. https://news.northwestern.edu/ stories/2015/03/ creative-genius-driven-by-distraction.

Harvard Business Review (2019). "The EI Advantage: Driving Innovation and Business Success through the Power of Emotional Intelligence." Accessed June 11, 2020. https://hbr.org/resources/pdfs/comm/fourseasons/ TheEIAdvantage.pdf.

DQ Institute (2015). "What Is DQ (Digital Intelligence)?" Accessed October 13, 2020. https://www.dqinstitute. org/ dq-framework/.

Cornell University (2015). Cornell University Digital Literacy resource: "Digital literacy is…." Retrieved from https:// digitalliteracy.cornell.edu/.

Star Trek Voyager. "Innocence." 1996. (Television.)

McKay, Brett, and McKay, Kate. *The Art of Manliness: Classic Skills and Manners for the Modern Man.* Simon & Schuster, 2009.

Drucker, Peter F. *The Effective Executive.* HarperCollins, 2006.

McKinsey & Company (2016). "Transforming operations management for a digital world." Accessed February 4, 2020. https://www.mckinsey.com/business-func- tions/ strategy-and-corporate-finance/our-insights/ how-covid-19-has-pushed-companies-over-the-technology-tipping-point-and-transformed-business-forever.

McKinsey & Company (2016). "The Next Normal Digitizing at speed and scale: The recovery will be digital." Accessed November 16, 2020. https://www.mckinsey.com/~/ media/McKinsey/Business%20Functions/McKinsey%20 Digital/Our%20Insights/How%20six%20companies%20 are%20using%20technology%20and%20data%20 to%20 transform%20themselves/The-next-normal-the-recovery-will-be-digital.pdf.

PART III: DELIVER IRRESISTIBLE VALUE EVERYWHERE

Munroe, Dr. Myles. *Becoming a Leader: How to Develop and Release Your Unique Gifts.* Whitaker House, 2018.

Harvard Business Review (2019). The EI Advantage: Unleashing Greatness in Others, accessed June 20, 2020. https:// hbr. org/webinar/2020/03/unleashing-greatness-in-others.

Rogers, David. *The Digital Transformation Playbook: Rethink Your Business for the Digital Age.* Columbia Business School Publishing, 2016.

Black Enterprise (2016). "4 Ways to Increase Your Value at Work." Accessed June 9, 2020. https://www.blackenterprise.com/increase-your-value-at-work/.

Harvard Business Review (2010). "Managing Yourself: Bringing Out the Best in Your People." Accessed July 13, 2020. https://hbr.org/2010/05/ managing-yourself-bringing-out-the-best-in-your-people.

Harvard Business Review (2016). "5 Ways to Instantly Increase Your Leadership Presence." Accessed April 8, 2020. https:// hbr.org/2016/09/the-elements-of-value.

Harvard Business Review (2018). "How to Increase Your Influence at Work." Accessed April 8, 2020. https:// hbr. org/2018/02/how-to-increase-your-influence-at-work.

CPSIA information can be obtained
at www.ICGtesting.com
Printed in the USA
BVHW060408231121
622231BV00014B/736